Kingdom Collision

The Movement of God's Spirit in a Time of War

JACK MILLER

CROSSBOOKS
PUBLISHING

CrossBooks™
A Division of LifeWay
1663 Liberty Drive
Bloomington, IN 47403
www.crossbooks.com
Phone: 1-866-879-0502

First published by CrossBooks 04/29/10

ISBN: 978-1-6150-7217-0 (sc)

Library of Congress Control Number: 2010905766

Printed in the United States of America
Bloomington, Indiana

This book is printed on acid-free paper.

Dedication

To Tina, my wife and friend: You exemplify grace and beauty, making our time together on earth a wonderful life.

To Dad: You showed me the value of hard word, and taught me the power of knowledge through reading. You always believed in me and I miss you.

To Franklin and the church family of West Ripley Baptist Church: Your faithful support and service to the Lord is greatly appreciated and is written in the ages. May there be many stars in your crown.

And to the members of the 64th Air Expeditionary Group, past, present and future: One Team, One Fight, One Mission. Thank you for your service to our great nation. May God bless you and protect you in all that you do.

Introduction

It was the last leg of the 27-hour flight home from Operation Enduring Freedom (OEF). I had completed five months in the desert; in less than 30 minutes I would finally be home.

Home. I had not thought much about home recently; I could not allow myself the luxury. It would have been too difficult, too stressful. I had to do the job that I was called to do; and I had to be 'All' there to do it. There would be no time for wishful thoughts longing for places I would have rather been. I could not allow my mind at any time to drift back to home or to even think about the future after the desert.

The Turbojet carried fewer than 15 passengers from Dulles International to Charleston, WV on this short flight; yet, it had been the roughest flight of the entire journey. From Riyadh to Heathrow in England, to Washington, D.C., the flight had been smooth and uneventful – until now. Now, the plane rocked and swayed through the sky with its small band of airborne travelers.

Looking through the clouds from my window seat, I saw mountains covered in green and valleys consumed with waterways; a welcomed sight after seeing only colors that were invariably some shade of tan or brown. Complaints about the rough ride raced through my mind but were brought to an end when I thought – "I'm in a recliner soaring through the sky." Amazing. God's gifts to mankind through technology, which we often take for granted, never cease to amaze me.

Next to me sat an attractive, twenty-something female; blonde hair, blue eyes and wearing a skirt that raised above her knees. This was very odd – for five months all women I had encountered had either the professional barrier of the Air Force uniform or the cultural barrier of full Islamic dress; both shouting a warning for all males to stay away. I looked down at my wedding band; its gold flashed as the sun moved through the window and I felt the irony of the situation. It didn't matter where I was in the world, no other woman truly catches my eye, for only one holds my heart.

As I looked at her and how she was dressed, I was taken aback. Her face being exposed and her attire wasn't inappropriate for America, but it was criminal in the Muslim world. I thought to myself, "If we were in the Kingdom, she would be arrested."

The Kingdom. A few months earlier those words meant something entirely different to me. 'The Kingdom' meant God's Kingdom or Christ's Kingdom to be established at His return. But now, 'the Kingdom' meant only one thing – The Kingdom of Saudi Arabia (KSA) - a place nearly 7,500 miles and 10 centuries away from my life at home in the United States.

After five months in KSA, I had changed and I knew it. Never before had I lived in a place whose leader was not elected; in KSA, a king ruled with the Divine Right of absolute authority. While our President's first responsibility is to act as the Commander-in-Chief, the King of Saudi Arabia's chief responsibility is to guard and protect the two holiest shrines of Islam – Mecca and Medina. Never before had I been to a place where Christianity was not the dominant religion, nor had I experienced life in a location where preaching the Gospel and evangelism was illegal, and in some cases, punishable by death. I had never even met one person of the 'Underground Church,' much less work with groups of these Christians as they lived under the threat of persecution. It was as if I had just stepped backward into time and then returned.

While I had never witnessed these things, I had also never experienced the power of God and His Spirit moving so strongly or being so active as I had in the Kingdom.

During my tour of duty, I had witnessed God move powerfully in and through the lives of civilians, underground saints, military men and women, and in my own life. And while the planes of the 130th Air Wing were a welcomed, joyful sight to my eyes as we landed, at the same time I was overwhelmed with a flood of mixed emotions. Emotions aside, when I stepped off of that small plane and onto the ramp, the very first thing I did was kneel down and thank God for what had happened in the Kingdom and for bringing me home safely.

I was truly thrilled and elated beyond words to be returning from the desert, to the arms of my wife, to the love and fellowship of my church family and to the solidarity of my unit. Yet, I was also overcome with a well-spring of sadness and emptiness, knowing what had happened and those whom I had left behind in the desert.

For one brief moment in time, I had been a part of something very, very special, not because of the unit with whom I was stationed, but because of the Lord whom I serve. It had been a life-changing experience; one for which I am truly thankful and blessed to have engaged in by God's Sovereign design. It was a once in a lifetime experience as His Spirit moved in the desert.

Chapter 1

ENTERING ESKAN

From thirty thousand feet above the desert floor below, all I could see was a vast darkness. The Kingdom of Saudi Arabia had been the fodder of myth and fables for centuries; it was now below me but the darkness did not add to its mystique. The journey had been long and tiring. I had spent my time reading Tom Brokaw's *The Greatest Generation* throughout the trip in the air. It had rained in America and snowed in Germany, but now, all I could see was darkness below and stars blanketing the night sky like diamonds on black velvet.

Most of the people on the plane were of Arab descent and dressed according to their culture. It was a far cry from the Europeans I had seen in Germany. I had finally received a seat with no one next to me, a pleasure considering I had spent seven hours across the North Atlantic squashed between two large Germans who didn't speak English. During that leg of the trip, I sat in the same position the entire time. With no one to talk to because I don't speak German, and with nowhere to go because I couldn't move, I simply read.

As we landed, I completed the entry card that was to be given to some official in customs. In bright, red letters and in three languages it warned at the top, "Possession of drugs is illegal in Saudi Arabia, punishable by death." I knew that this would be someone's one and only warning, thinking, "I bet they don't have too many problems with drug addicts." I was right.

Passengers began to shift and move off the plane; I stuck the card in my shirt pocket for later use. I didn't want to carry that big book through customs or into the country, so I stuck it in the seat pouch in front of me, silently hoping that some European would read it and realize what my countrymen of a generation ago did for their countrymen and maybe be thankful for the sacrifice for liberty.

Somewhere on this plane was my assistant, TSgt Claudette Arms. We had been separated earlier in the flight and I was hoping she didn't journey too far away in the airport. In Saudi Arabia, including King Khalid International Airport (KKIA), it was illegal for a female to be alone in public.

Also on this flight was LTC Richard Wagner, the in-coming commander of Eskan Services Squadron (ESS). I had no idea what he looked like, but I imagined that his haircut would give him away and make him recognizable; that happens to most military personnel traveling in civilian attire.

After finding Claudette, we traveled through KKIA, attempting to be as culturally aware as possible. She wore the Abaya, a head covering required for females in KSA. She also walked several paces behind me, never spoke, and did not make eye contact with anyone as we passed through the airport. While we didn't necessarily agree with all the cultural practices of this region, neither of us wanted to cause an international incident only a few minutes after arrival.

As we approached the port of entry into KSA and the lines where people were entering the country through customs, I was introduced to an entirely new concept – Third Country Nationals or TCNs. The entry point was packed with TCNs, people who had come from other Third World nations to work in Saudi Arabia. What they didn't realize until they arrived was the fact that a TCN in this country was nothing more than a virtual slave.

For a TCN to come to Saudi Arabia as a worker, he or she had to first have an employer who would sponsor them so that they would be able to enter the country. To enter Saudi Arabia a person must have a reason for being there such as government work, private employer or a religious purpose such as the Hajj. There are no tourists in Saudi Arabia. A private employer would sponsor their contracted TCN. Rarely did I see a Saudi national doing actual 'work' outside of a military or government position. They hired TCNs for nearly all jobs, such as, construction, truck drivers, maids, restaurant help, etc. In America, the jobs a teenager or minimum wageworkers are hired to do were filled by TCNs in KSA. In Saudi Arabia, the working class was not the Saudi nationals, they were TCNs, and their pay topped off at approximately $150 a month.

In any case, when a TCN entered the Kingdom, it was common for their employer to confiscate their passport; which means they couldn't leave the country without their employer's permission. If the employer treated the TCN unfairly, there was little legal recourse he could take because the TCN had virtually no civil rights, protections or liberties.

Seeing the long line of TCNs made me cringe because I thought we would have to wait in line for hours before we could be processed. It was at this time a man in a military style uniform, carrying an AK-47 approached me and began giving me instructions in Arabic and pointing in a certain direction. It looked as if we had been directed down a corridor; I thought we were on the verge of being detained. In the direction he was pointing were several men dressed like he was and armed with the same weapons.

As we began walking in the direction of the corridor, an elderly Saudi Arabian with a long beard and kind eyes stopped me. He was trying to explain something to me, pointing in the direction of another line through customs. His one word of English told me all I needed to know: "wife." What I didn't know was that in Saudi Arabia, all public places have services separated by the distinction of "family" and "single men," similar to the American "smoking" and "non-smoking." It seemed that both he and the soldier were trying to tell me that I was to go through the "family" line of customs; they believed that Claudette and I were husband and wife, and we weren't going to tell them any different. Later, we would joke about this event, but at the time, we weren't laughing because we were on edge over the situation.

After going through customs, we were hit with a barrage of taxi drivers offering to take us wherever we were going. I knew the base was sending a driver, so I politely refused; the truth of it is, I didn't know where I was going so they would have been of little help anyway. Waiting to be identified by someone from the base began to be uncomfortable; we were beginning to get glaring looks from men dressed in all white thobes and head wraps. A "thobe" is the Saudi Arabian male version of what we would call a "robe," but in their culture, only females wear robes. Later I would learn that these men were members of the Mutawwa, the Saudi Arabian religious police.

Out of the crowd I heard a voice say, "Hey, Chaplain, how was the flight?" It was SSgt John Shank, a member of the 130th Air Wing from Charleston, West Virginia, my home unit. I said, "Please don't use that title out here." He smiled and cracked a chuckle under his breath, but I wasn't joking. I was fully aware of what they do to Christians in this country and I wanted to be sure to keep my head on my shoulders.

Shank looked different than he did when I had last seen him. He was in civilian clothes and had a beard; he looked almost Amish. At first, I didn't recognize him, but that was a good thing. He was part of the base Security Escort Team (SET), and part of their job was to blend in with the locals. He had done a magnificent job of looking like the locals, and I may not have known who he was at first, but I was sure glad to see him arrive.

He had us stand near a pillar as we waited on LTC Wagner to arrive through customs. Once all three of us were together and small introductions were made, we were loaded up in a van and headed to Eskan Village Air Base. I didn't have much time with Wagner that night, but in the months ahead, we would form a personal and professional relationship that I truly cherished in the desert.

The only way to describe the ride to the base is fast and furious. I didn't have the courage to look at the speedometer that night, but we were moving at a high rate as we weaved in and out of the heavy traffic. Without question, that ride was the most dangerous ride I had experienced in my life up to that point, but that would be nothing compared to the trips to the Embassy I would make in the days ahead.

"Welcome to Eskatraz." These were the first words I heard driving up to the gate of Eskan Village Air Base. It was a reference to the famed California prison and the daily repetitive lifestyle of those who occupied the base. All I could see were guards, gates, razor wire and walls. Shank was right, it did look like a prison from this perspective.

Pulling through the first and second gates were Saudi Nationals in red berets; they were members of the Saudi Arabian National Guard, who served at the will and pleasure of the King. They waved us through without incident. At the third gate my spirit perked up; the men in full battle gear were men from the 130th. Even though I recognized some of them, I didn't know them well, but just knowing there were other people there from Charleston helped me relax a little.

As we drove across base, the one thing in the darkness that I noticed was that there were no airplanes. I had assumed that every air base would have a flight line and airplanes; not true, but I found it odd anyway.

Tradition at Eskan Village was for the new arrivals to be dropped off at the Dining Facility parking lot, where members of their shop would pick them up and take them to their quarters. As we pulled into the lot, I saw a huge group of people there waiting for our arrival. It would later be these people with whom I would have the most effective ministry during my time in the desert. I just didn't know it at the time. Quick introductions were made; with handshakes and talk about flight times in getting there. Then a man wearing oak clusters on his collar walked up to me and said, "I'm Chaplain Rick Bach, welcome to Eskan Village."

It was 08 January 2009, and I was the replacement for Chaplain Bach, who had served since September of the previous year. Instantly, I had become his best friend in the entire world; my arrival meant that he could finally go home.

Chapter 2

Acclamation

With his Maine accent, Chaplain Bach said, "…and this is your room," smiling as he opened the door. I was stunned – not just at the room, but the entire set up. I wasn't standing in a tent or a barracks; I was standing in a villa with multiple rooms. My new quarters were a house complete with a kitchen and washer and dryer. Many men who are deployed to the desert must make use of "Cadillacs," which are portable showers and latrines. I was blessed enough to find myself at Eskan Village where my villa contained the coveted prize of bathrooms inside the house itself.

While three men would live there for several days, once Chaplain Bach and his assistant left, I would be living alone. This was a feature only four other men had on base: the Unit Commander and the two Squadron Commanders, and the highest ranking enlisted man, a Chief Master Sergeant. After a quick call to Tina, whom I affectionately refer to as my "smokin' hot wife," I was ready to hit the rack. I had not slept since I had left the United States a day and half before.

It was Chaplain Bach's responsibility to get me acclimated to my job as the chaplain before he left. For the next several days I would walk around in a jet lag fog and the information would come constantly. My job was to act like a sponge and absorb as much as I could about the host nation, the people, the military situation and my responsibilities while in theatre. This time of transition would be a luxury to any civilian pastor entering a new church; in the theatre of war during our day and age, this practice of overlapping with an individual's replace is an absolute necessity. Almost immediately I recognized how important this time period would be, knowing that I would soon be the only Christian minister within the Kingdom of Saudi Arabia.

Chaplain Miller, TSGT Arms: First Day in KSA

The next morning was Thursday and at Eskan Village which meant Men's Bible Study. This would have been fine except it was held at 0730. Even though I wanted to sleep in after such a long trip, at the appointed time I was ready to go. It was bright and early on that Thursday morning when I learned that I would have a car assigned to me for my use on base. I also learned that the base was divided into two sides: a permanent party side and a rotation side, of which I was a member. At the time, this meant absolutely nothing to me, but it became clear very soon that the two sides of the base played by two separate sets of rules while using the same sandbox.

The Bible study was held in a private villa on base which belonged to one of the permanent party contractors, a civilian and his wife – Rick and Nancy Jackson. Like many of the contractors on base, Rick former military. I found Rick and his wife to be two Godly people whom I would soon grow to appreciate very deeply. After retiring from the Air Force as a pilot, Rick and Nancy had worked and lived at Eskan for years, all the while being the backbone of the chapel community.

Afterwards, Chaplain Bach brought me back to the office and gave me the break down of the mission and the responsibility of the Chaplain at Eskan Village. Sitting at a conference table in the Chapel office, Bach explained through a Powerpoint Presentation that things were more complex than what they seemed on the surface.

King Abdullah had built Eskan Village years ago for the purpose of relocating the Bedouin tribes from the desert wilderness to this compound and others like it throughout Saudi Arabia. The King decided that it wasn't good for these nomadic tribes and their herds to be wandering through the desert; the building of these villages was a gesture of kindness from the King of the holiest land in the Muslim world. Interestingly enough, the Bin-Laden Group, a construction company, built Eskan Village. It would be this same Bin-Laden family whose offspring would produce Osama Bin-laden, the man responsible for the terrorist attacks of September 11th and the leader of Al-Qaida. In any case, the Bedouins came to Eskan with their herds of camels and goats, stayed only a short while and decided that life in these compounds was not for them and headed back to the wilderness of the desert. For all practical purposes, Eskan Village was abandoned until Operation Desert Shield, and later Desert Storm. As Saddam Hussein sat with seven divisions on the Kuwait/Saudi border, the United States sent troops to aid our ally in their time of need; the King offered Eskan and other compounds similar to it, to the American forces for use during the operation. By the time I had reached Eskan, the mission had changed and the people had changed, but the signs of a larger contingency were still present.

Today, Bach explained, Eskan Village had an invisible line dividing the base according to where the various military missions were located. One side of the base held the permanent party, which consisted of three different missions encompassing all four branches of the service. The mission groups were the Office of the Program Manager – Saudi Arabian National Guard (OPM-SANG), the Office of the Program Manager – Security Forces Squadron (OPM-SFS) and the largest of the three, the United States Military Training Mission (USMTM). Interestingly enough,

USMTM is the largest such training mission in the world outside of the borders of the United States. Together, their mission was to train Saudi nationals in military techniques and tactics, as well as selling the Saudi government military equipment and weapons.

On the other side of the base was the 64th Air Expeditionary Group (64 AEG), containing only Air Force personnel. This was the unit to which I was attached during my tour of duty. The mission was simple, Force Protection; the members of the 64 AEG were to defend the base from threats of aggression or terrorism. The nature of the mission explained why there weren't any airplanes. The Air Force didn't fly missions from this base, the Air Force was to protect the base from enemy combatants so that USMTM and the other groups could carry out their mission of training the nationals.

The 64th AEG was far more restricted than the other side of the base. We were to be in uniform at all times, while the permanent party could wear civilian clothes when not on duty. Members of the 64th could not go off base at any time, with only exception being that the member was one of a handful of people who had a reason to be off base to fulfill their job assignment; I was one of them.

Chaplain Bach explained that in addition to the chapel services on base, I would also be responsible for the services at the U.S. Embassy in downtown Riyadh. The reason was simple: I would be the only minister in the entire country. The 64 AEG Chaplain provided for the religious needs of the civilians and the small band of Marines at the Embassy. Later, I would obtain a diplomatic ID card to gain access and move freely in the Embassy.

As I sat there listening, I was beginning to feel overwhelmed. I was beginning to have doubts about my ability to function effectively as the lone "pastor/chaplain" for such diverse groups of people. Yet, a simple truth from the hand of the Apostle Paul, written centuries before, echoed through my soul: "I can do all things through Christ who strengthens me." I knew the Holy Spirit had brought this simple verse back to my mind and I knew those words were from the very mind of God Himself; all I had to do was have enough faith in that truth and the Lord who had given it, regardless of what might lay ahead in the days to come.

As my education concerning the mission went forward, Chaplain Bach explained to me the chain-of-command structure, which differed on each side of the base. There were two separate command structures that did not overlap one another, at times, he explained, this would be a source of tension between the commanding officers. He also taught me about the regular duties, the paperwork, the responsibilities and what was expected from the chaplain. I also learned that Chaplain Bach had a minimum of 50 hours of visitation every week and had never taken a day off the entire time he had been deployed in theatre. Here was genuine man of God who had ministered effectively and thoroughly, giving of himself constantly and taking care of his "people" wonderfully; however, the one person he had not cared for was himself. Every minister must take time to rest and replenish his soul spiritually and his body physically, regardless is the person is military or civilian. Many ministers feel as if there is no time to rest because in our minds there are "just too many things to do." As a result, we become the losers in our relationships with our families and our Lord. We would do well to listen to the Lord Jesus Christ when He said, "Sabbath was created for man, not man for the Sabbath."

The day came and went while I was still in a jet lag fog. The next day was Friday and I would see what the chaplain was to do through two services and an evening social. The "weekend" in Saudi Arabia is Thursday and Friday; Friday being the Sabbath. We often called it virtual Sunday; we treated Friday as Sunday and our calendars on base reflected this pattern.

Friday morning I met a priest on base coming out of a worship service and headed to the Embassy. That is when I learned that the 379th Air Wing in Qatar, to which we were attached, sent a priest once every two to three weeks to minister to the Catholics on base and downtown at the Embassy. After his service, he returned to Qatar and we began our service for the Protestants.

An hour prior to the Protestant service was Friday School; it was Sunday School on Friday. Friday School was held in the kitchen of what was called the Breezeway, located on the USMTM side of the base. The Breezeway consisted of long, open corridors with shops on either side of the corridor. As I walked through the Breezeway, I saw that there was a barber, a massage therapist, a tailor, and what we called the "Saudi Seven-Eleven." But it was in Breezeway meeting room number 2 that the service would be held.

When I entered, the singing struck me; it was powerful, passionate and consisted of several men who were simply praising God with the talents with which He had blessed them. The music was more modern than my home church, but excellent. It became one of my small joys to listen to these men sing as they rehearsed every Friday morning before service began.

Praise Band at Breezeway Service

After the service, Chaplain Bach and several from the congregation went to the Eskan Community Club (ECC), a restaurant of sorts on the USMTM side of base. It was nice, but later I would find it too difficult with the time restraints of going to the embassy to eat there very often after service. It was much easier, although less exciting, to opt for the food at the Dining Facility (DFAC).

Returning to the Villa, we quickly changed into civilian clothes and met the SET team for transport to the Embassy. The SET team would be our armed escorts anytime we needed to go off base. In the daylight I could see more outside of the Eskan walls than razor wire and roads. Amazingly, I learned that the desert was cluttered with filth. Along the razor wire and the walls, so much trash piled up that it nearly prevented us from seeing the sand. Debris was constantly blowing into the wire and getting caught in it due to the desert winds; I truly believe that is the place where plastic bags go to die.

Two nights earlier when I had arrived at Eskan, I had noticed a odor in the air; now, I realized why. Garbage was everywhere: on the roads, in the desert; the place was simply full of trash. To make matters worse, people of that region burn anything that can burn: tires, paper, used oil; if it could be burned, it would be burned. There is no Environmental Protection Agency in Saudi Arabia.

Another enlightening revelation about this trip to the embassy was the manner in which people drive in Saudi Arabia. I had been at some high speeds and driven on dangerous roads in the past, but it was nothing like what I was now experiencing. Our drivers were excellent in their alertness and skill; however, the local custom is to run the engine full throttle. It was nothing to top the odometer off at 130 mph. Amazingly, there were no seat belt or child restraint laws. Many times we would watch other cars pass us doing 90 to 100 mph, with gaping mouths as they traveled with infants crawling across the dashboard. Once, we were headed to the embassy and a Toyota passed us. This wasn't unusual except for the fact that his front bumper was hanging out the back seat window on the driver's side of the car. In short, if it could be driven, it was; and if it could be driven on, they did. Occasionally, we would pass a truck hauling a camel in the back. I have often wondered what the life expectancy is of a camel on the streets of Riyadh, Saudi Arabia.

At the Embassy, I met the group of believers there for the very first time; it was a smaller group than what I had expected. Most of them worked on the embassy grounds in some capacity; yet, there was one family who were escorted in by a worker every week. This man would become a dear friend; later I learned that he was a pastor of one of the Underground Churches in Saudi. It is for this reason he will remain nameless.

This would be Chaplain Bach's last visit to the embassy. This small group of believers held a going-away party; each one making a food that was native to their nation of origin. This fellowship of believers was sincere; fully understanding what the treasure of the Gospel meant; worshipping secretly under the threat of persecution. There were several nationalities from around the globe represented in this group; some spoke English very well, but others did not. Skin tones and accents varied among these men and women, but our differences meant very little. As we came together in worship, in the fellowship of Christ, there was a genuine bond of love and a spirit of unity that one rarely finds.

As things wrapped up, Bach said his good-byes and this small band of believers welcomed me with open arms and open hearts. As we began our return journey to Eskan, I began to feel slightly ill, but I shrugged it off as part of the jet lag experience.

That night was Bach's final social gathering on the rooftop of the chapel office. He held many during his time at Eskan, and for good reason. A previous rotation had somehow received thousands of dollars from the commander at the time and renovated the rooftop as a prayer garden complete with tables, chairs, fans, and a running fountain. It was a great place to gather for fellowship, and it would be on this rooftop that I would get my first real interaction with the members of the chapel community. It would also be on this roof, several days later, when I would make a promise to myself and to the Lord about the ministry He had given me at Eskan Village.

The night events began to wind down and people were slowly leaving. By now, I wasn't feeling well at all. I returned to the villa and I was very sick. That night I barely slept; time seemed to pass so slowly. The next morning I was up and ready; I had not been in the office ten minutes and I found myself on my knees before the porcelain god Earl in the latrine. When I came out, Bach's assistant looked at me with compassion in his eyes and said, 'Sir, you need to go to sick call.'

So, off to sick call I went, soon having a IV in my arm and nurses feeling sorry for me. The flight doc gave me phenergan, which I must admit is a wonderful drug; yet, the major side effect of phenergan is that it makes you sleep – a lot. I slept the entire day. To this day, I have no idea what transpired that day in the desert, but I know that I wasn't a part of it. In the evening, I rose for about an hour, ate a Popsicle and drank a bottle of Gatorade, took another phenergan and then slept the entire night. When I awoke the next morning, I felt certain my body was adjusted to the time change.

My first Sunday in the desert brought the reality of spiritual weight in the responsibility of being the chaplain at Eskan. I had watched Bach in action, Claudette had learned her role as the assistant, and we both knew how to produce the required paperwork, but there was more to this than met the eye. Chaplain Bach sat me down in the office and said I would have a security briefing in a couple of days, but there was more that I needed to know than what I would be told.

He told me that as the chaplain, I had a price on my head by the Mutawwa; not because of who I was, but what I am: a Christian minister. It is not illegal to be a Christian in Saudi Arabia; we are considered to be "the People of the Book." It is however illegal to propagate the Gospel and to convert to Christianity, punishable by death.

Not long before I arrived in KSA, a 13 year-old girl had been publicly beheaded; her crime was confessing Jesus Christ as Lord and renouncing Islam. The worst part of the whole scenario was the fact that her own parents had reported her and turned her over to the Mutawwa. When she refused to denounce her new faith after being "interrogated," the young girl's life was ended in front of cheering crowds before it ever began. In the back of my mind, I thought of how spoiled many American Christians are today; most will go to their graves without ever sharing Christ. This young girl died proclaiming Christ.

My mind drifted briefly on this matter, when Bach asked me if I had any questions for him. I had noticed a room stacked full of food, clothes and supplies in the villa, but I didn't know why. I said, 'Major, what is all that stuff in the extra bedroom at the villa?'

He looked at me with a seriousness in his eyes and said, "It's for a battered women's shelter. We have collected these supplies for over a month now; you will have more come in before it goes to them. He told me that very few knew about the shelter and that we shouldn't broadcast the information; in time, he said, someone would get in touch with me about it.

A women's shelter for abused women? In Saudi Arabia? And we have to be secretive about this? Who wouldn't want to help them? It made absolutely no sense to me at the time, but as I learned more about Saudi Arabia and the culture, eventually it would all make perfect sense.

Chapter 3

Preach the Word

I stood on the rooftop watching the sun rise above Eskan Village, slowly changing the hue of the sky and warming the air around me. It was my first day. The night before, Chaplain Bach had held his last service, got ready, went to the parking lot amid many well-wishers and left for Maine. He had given me 100 Saudi Riyals (sr100), or "Rips", and an Italian made tie. The money was to get me started if I needed anything before I had my Eagle Cash Card set up. An Eagle Card is a debit card system used in theatre. It was a thoughtful gesture from a thoughtful man.

The breeze was ever so slight against my face; warm to be so early in the morning, after all, it was January. At 0500 the Islamic call to prayer had sounded throughout the land, with all the faithful bowing and praying toward Mecca. They are truly a faithful people; and yet, they are truly lost. I knew I wasn't there to win the entire country to Christ in one single blow; my mission was the base below me, now beginning to awaken to activity. And that was when a light engulfed my soul and changed my outlook from that day forward in the desert.

Up to that point, coming straight from a local church pastorate, I had been worried about Air Force responsibility and chaplain-style ministry; failing to realize they were one and the same. Chaplain Bach truly loved the people, had formed wonderful relationships, excelled in visitation and preached relationally. I knew there was no way I was going to match him in these areas. Then it hit me: "Just be who you are," a simple, yet profound truth. I am a Southern Baptist preacher; that is who I am, and that was exactly what I would do – preach the Word.

I knew I was called to Eskan by the Divine hand of God. I also knew that I would have only one shot, one chance, one opportunity, to rightly and effectively communicate the Gospel of Christ on this base at this time. Whatever else would happen, I was going to take that one shot no matter what. Regardless of who might be in the services or where I would be preaching in this Kingdom, I would preach and live the Gospel for His Kingdom. The setting was different, the people were different and the ministry was different, but the Gospel is never-changing and eternal.

That morning I had my first one-on-one meeting with the Commander of the 64th AEG. I had heard stories from other chaplains about some commanders not placing too much value on what the chaplain corps does; at this point I didn't know what to expect. These meetings would be held in my office weekly, not his. In the chain-of-command, I reported directly to the base commander, ensuring direct line of communication from my office to his.

In these meetings, I would report what I was doing and how the troops seemed to be fairing and if there were any personal circumstances of the troops that might impede the mission – without giving names or breaking confidence. Some commanders might press other chaplains for details, but that was never an issue at any time with any commander I served with at Eskan Village.

Colonel Talentino Anglesante was the first base commander I would serve with in the 64th. He was a very unique man and had years of combat experience. He had been raised a Catholic, but with his unique sense of humor, he spent several months trying to convince me he was a Buddhist. I don't think either of us ever bought into it.

The Commander had two major concerns – the mission and the men; these are the two concerns that any commander worth his salt ought to have. If there was anything I could do to help morale or support our airmen, he made it clear that he would support my efforts. Later, he would make good on that pledge. Not once did he ever turn down a request that I made for an event, a service, a social or money I requested to support chapel events. And that was something I truly appreciated in him.

During that day and the following, I mapped out c
service and every message I would preach during my
there would be unexpected events or special days p
that if I could prepare for what I knew was comi
unexpectedly, I wouldn't have to worry about the regular ac
could concentrate on those unexpected interruptions. At this point, I could
prepare for everything I knew about because most people were allowing
me a couple of day's adjustment time.

I felt led and made the decision that every service would be different:
different music, different order of service and different messages preached,
but all would have solid, Biblical doctrine. On virtual Sundays (Friday
mornings) at the Breezeway and Embassy, the messages would be the
same because the two groups would never interact with one another. The
messages would concern various Biblical and doctrinal topics but the music
at the two locations would be tailored to the preferences of these two vastly
different groups of people.

In addition to Friday service on base, there were two other services:
Sunday Night at the Oasis of Peace Chapel and on Wednesday evening,
also at the chapel. I knew that there would be some who would go to
all three services. With Friday decided, Sunday nights would take on a
contemporary flavor with music; the musicians in this service loved the
contemporary style. The messages would center on the lives of the apostles
first, then other Biblical characters as the tour of duty drew to a close. On
Wednesday evenings, I felt led to teach about the women of the Bible, who
I have always felt get short-changed in our Bible Studies and teachings.
But the point of it all was to have solid teaching, to preach Biblical truth,
and to show that Biblical men and women that we often revere as "super
saints" weren't really much different than we are; rather, it was the Holy
Spirit within them which allowed them to accomplish all they did for the
Lord.

As time went forward, with the varied music and messages, the
visitation, the base involvement and being a split-gender chapel team, I
truly believed we would be able to reach out to nearly every person on
that base. Our charge from the commander had been to be "visible and
available," and I believed we were heading in the right direction. With my
office phone linked with my room phone, carrying a cell phone, and being
in the center of the base, I was always available anywhere I went in Saudi
Arabia. We were also always visible, meaning that we didn't stay in the
office, but got out in the heat among the troops. I believed at the time that

were reaching our chapel arms across the base and no shop of airmen would be missed; however, the reality of it was that we were over looking a very important group of people.

Not long after I arrived at Eskan, I had visited the main gate at night. It was here that I had seen members of the 130th when I arrived. Several of those airmen came to me in the chapel office one day after that visit and said that none of them had been to church in nearly three months. The problem was when the existing services were held, they were either working or sleeping. Then one of them asked, "We've got a couple of people who will play the music. Would you mind starting up a service for the night shift earlier in the morning so we can go to church?" Without hesitation I said, "Absolutely."

The time was set for 0800 on Sunday mornings, and the commander quickly approved, sending out a memo instructing all supervisors to allow any person on any shift to be relieved of their responsibilities for one hour if they wanted to go to this new service. He told me later that he didn't realize these airmen were being missed; neither had I, nor had Chaplain Bach. A chaplain's chief responsibility after glorifying and honoring God is simple: to provide the means by which the military service member may engage in their Constitutional right of the free exercise of religion. There was no way either of us, nor anyone else on that base, was going to deny this request.

With the advent of a fifth worship service on a weekly basis, I would be preparing four different preaching messages a week, a feat unheard of in the local church pastorate with regards to sermon preparation. In total, our chapel team would be responsible for five services and three Bible studies a week. Over the course of being deployed for 126 days, I would preach 91 different sermons in Saudi Arabia.

It is my sincere belief that no human being has that much of value to say nor are they worth listening to that much in and of themselves. I knew then, as I know now, for this ministry to be successful, the Holy Spirit of God would have to empower me and be the ministering agent at Eskan Village.

Only a few days passed before I truly began to feel the Holy Spirit's power and the hand of God guiding this ministry. What I did not expect was the immediate response from heaven; often I have found we pray and then don't expect God to move. As a result, He doesn't. But He moved swiftly in my life at Eskan. In the pastorate, I had dealt with various counseling issues with men and women; but those were local, American church issues and problems. In the desert, I had to come face-to-face with the saddest and maybe the most difficult situation any deployed person can deal with from the home front: "Dear John" letters.

I cannot begin to describe the compassion I felt for the men in the field who received these from their wives; nor can I accurately describe my personal disgust for those who sent them. The number of people whom faced this problem was quite large, given the fact we were a small base. Most were younger men in their early 20's, deployed for the first time; only to find out their selection for a wife had been disastrous. Some had their homes and checking accounts wiped out; others had simply been notified of adultery by email. All of them had one thing in common: they were absolutely devastated.

With each of them, my thoughts would naturally and briefly return to my own home, my wife, and my children. In the desert, regardless of how strong an individual's marriage might be, Satan uses your mind against you and your thoughts begin to linger because you see so many marriages fall to pieces. The reality of it was that not everybody has married a woman of high quality and integrity as I have. As I listened to these broken men with broken hearts and homes, I knew the foundation of my marriage was solid; for it was not pieced together by a faith in one another, but by our mutual faith in Christ.

At times, I would feel guilty knowing that I would eventually go home and get on with life with my family. Some of these men would have no home to go to. My marriage has had its ups and downs over the years; but I have no regrets in marrying Tina. I know she was created for me and given to me by the hand of God. For this, I am and will remain eternally thankful.

I can remember listening to these men, walking with them, praying with them, and at times, holding them as they wept. It was hard on them and I hated it – not my part in trying to minister to them, but in the fact they had to go through the turmoil. Had I not asked for God's empowerment, grace and guidance through His Spirit, I truly do not believe I could have been of any help to them at all.

In that moment of time, each of them carried on and went forward with the mission. As for what happened when they returned, I do not know; the end of those tales are written in the ages. Yet, I do have a peace in my Spirit when each one of these men is brought to my mind today. I can only trust that the same Spirit that guided me then guided their actions and decisions when they returned home – just as we had prayed in the desert.

```
Chapter 4
```

What I Didn't Expect

"Friends, I'm a Southern Baptist preacher; that's what I do…" Those were the first words I spoke at the first service I held at Eskan Village. A slight chuckle rippled across the congregation, but the preaching ministry came easy for me. Whether I was in the Breezeway or at the Chapel, I would preach until I was finished and then gave an invitation – every time. The invitation part of the service was a new concept for some; past chaplains didn't have a regular invitation at the end of the service and some of the people who attended the services came from faith traditions that do not give altar calls. But how can a person respond to the Word of God if they aren't given the opportunity? I had decided, that while I was at Eskan, the congregation would have an opportunity to respond.

Preaching, visitation and counseling are only part of the chaplain's vast role at Eskan Village. Being the only chaplain in the entire country and serving both sides of the base meant that I was regularly called on to do special activities; at times it seemed that I was the only person on base who had the ability to pray publicly. Invocations and benedictions at social events, retirements, promotions and formal ceremonies became quite frequent. I knew there would be times when I was called upon to do these duties; I just did not realize how often they would come.

The very first official act that I did as "the chaplain" was a change-of-command ceremony for LTC Wagner as the incoming commander of ESS. The morning the ceremony took place was the coolest day I experienced in the desert and it was the only time I wore a jacket. I was nervous and I didn't want to mess up the ceremony steeped in tradition and before the entire 64th AEG, with USMTM's commanders and Host Nation dignitaries present. So I wrote the prayer on a small piece of paper and stuck it in my pocket. After the prayer was finished, I walked off the platform and placed it back in the jacket. Months later, after I had returned home, I put the coat on and felt the prayer still inside the jacket, bringing back fond memories of the people I had met and the things I had experienced.

LTC Wagner was a hard charger and a hard worker, expecting the same for those who served under him. Although I could never defeat him in table tennis, he made the desert a better place for everyone. He had been raised Catholic, but often came with his men to the Sunday night Protestant service. Before we left the desert, he told me that I was the best preacher/chaplain he'd ever sat under in church and had learned more in our chapel services than in years at his church. That was one of the highest and most cherished compliments I have ever received.

Along with LTC Wagner's ceremony, I performed two more change-of-command events. The first was for USMTM, in which Major General Van Sickle took command; it was an Air Force General replacing an Army General Officer. Being such an important mission in that region of the world, this was a huge event in terms of attendance and ceremony. Distinguished Visitors (DVs) from Central Command were present, as were commanders from the Host Nation's military. It was a beautiful spring day when the authority of USMTM was given to General Van Sickle, but what I remember most was his presence at the ceremony itself. Even though I met with them only briefly among a crowd of well-wishers, both he and his wife seemed to be very humble and gracious.

The next change-of-command came with the transfer of the 64th AEG to Colonel Mike Hatcher. He was a fellow Air Guardsman from Tennessee; as with the previous commander, we had weekly meetings and I got to know him fairly well.

A note of praise should be mentioned at this point. When my ministry began at Eskan, not one of the commanders on base participated in the chapel services. By the time I had left the desert, all but one could be found in at least one of the various services on base throughout the week.

As each one began to come, I realized that God's Spirit was beginning to stir hearts in KSA.

The first social event at which I was to give the invocation was the Eskan community's celebration of Black History Month. When contacted about attending and taking part in the event, I felt odd. No one knew that I had been raised in an area where everyone, and I literally mean everyone, was white. I did not go to school with a person of another race until I was in college. In fact, where I currently pastor, there are only a handful of African-Americans in the entire county. When I agreed to be at this event, I thought, "I'm going to be so out of place." But that wasn't how it turned out to be.

Typically with social events and AF ceremonies, the chaplain is seated in the front near the guest of honor, among dignitaries or with those of high rank. This was the case at Eskan Village with all events; however, I did not know this until I arrived. I arrived early thinking I could choose a seat in the back of the room and if I felt uncomfortable or out of place, I would quietly slip away. Much to my surprise, that just wasn't going to happen because I was sitting in the middle of a raised platform above the crowd, at a table with an army full-bird colonel. As I look back on the event, I am so glad that I was able to be a part of that special celebration. This event turned out to be one of the high points of my deployment.

The organizers had brought in authentic tribal dancers from Africa to perform. Some recited poems, while others performed in a drama; not only was this entertaining but it was also informative. Far from being uncomfortable, I truly enjoyed myself. I think many times we limit God's blessing on our lives by not going out of our normal procedures in life and trying new and different things, even though we might be skeptical about them. I was in a position where I had to go to this event and I am so thankful that I did because God blessed me during the celebrations.

There were two other events which I am so thankful to have been a part of at Eskan. The first was Eskan Village's farewell to the United States' Ambassador to the Kingdom of Saudi Arabia, Ford M. Fraker. The second was a ceremony to celebrate the 1977 Peace Accord agreement with KSA.

As is political tradition, when a new President assumes office, new ambassadors are appointed to help steer our nation's foreign policy goals in line with the new administration. That night, I had dinner with the ambassador, with many others in attendance. As he spoke, he reminded us how important the United States relationship is with the Kingdom of

Saudi Arabia as our ally in the region and as our supporter within OPEC. Soon, a new ambassador would arrive and continue building the ties our two nations had forged in the past. Before he left, I asked him, "Mr. Ambassador, might I have a picture taken with you to send home to my wife?" He readily agreed, and just before it was snapped, LTC Wagner joined us. Afterwards, I saw a print of the photo only once and to this day I have no idea where it might be.

The next important event was the celebration of the signing of the 1977 Peace Accords. Each year the USMTM and the Royal Saudi Arabian Naval Forces as well as the Saudi Arabian Ministry of Defense and Aviation meet at Eskan Village to celebrate this anniversary. At this event, both nations also recognize individuals in their achievements in promoting stronger bonds between the two nations.

The celebration was held outdoors and I arrived early. When I saw the multitude of chairs, I knew the event was more significant than I had realized. Soon, Saudi dignitaries and Royal Princes in full traditional dress began to arrive. It was at this point that I realized that I had to be very cautious when I spoke and gave the invocation.

When I was sworn into the Air Force, I was hired as a Christian minister. At any event, I am expected to function as a Christian minister. At this event, I was expected to pray. Normally I would pray and close the prayer by saying, '...we ask these things in the name of Jesus Christ, Amen,' or something very similar. I knew that I could do that on this occasion and there would be no repercussions; however, I also knew that I needed to be culturally sensitive to the Saudi Muslims who were present.

It is no secret that since the beginning of the Global War on Terror, many Islamic militants have viewed the United States as being enjoined in a modern day crusade. It is also true that the Kingdom of Saudi Arabia has been our chief ally in that region of the world, although there have been some tense situations in recent years. The last thing I wanted to do was to add to that tension by angering or offending our Host Nation dignitaries who were present, but I also knew that I needed to remain faithful to Christ.

I had become quite comfortable in praying before the men and women of our Air Base; I no longer used notes to prompt me. When I stepped up to the podium, I had no idea how I was going to end the prayer. I began by thanking God for our working relationship with the Kingdom, the peace that He alone provides, the safety and security which all had enjoyed – but I still didn't know how to end this prayer. It would have been easy just to say, "in the name of God" or "in Your name…" or something generic; but I didn't feel that would have been right. This was a very unique situation to say the least. I have heard many civilian pastors boldly say what they would do in this type of situation, but I doubt they will ever find themselves in this situation. It is much easier to say what you are "going to do" when you will never be in a position to do it.

Just before I closed the prayer, I did something that many won't do. I paused. Most people would just plow through the situation and let the cards fall wherever they may; I couldn't do that. This was too important and had wider implications than just for the time I would be in the desert. When I paused, the Spirit gave me these words: "…and Almighty God, we pray these things and ask your blessings from this kingdom as we await your eternal Kingdom on earth, Amen."

As we lifted our heads, one of the members of the chapel community was smiling ear-to-ear, knowing what I had just struggled with in those few brief moments. The Saudi's also lifted their heads, smiling to one another. After this, the celebration went on and people were honored for their achievements – international incident avoided. It was a good day.

Chapter 5

The Underground

Repetition. It is the surest enemy of a deployed soldier, sailor, airman or marine because repetition gives birth to boredom. At Eskan, we referred to our repetition as "Ground Hog Day;" a reference to the movie in which the lead character relives February 2nd over and over again. Many who have been deployed can easily identify with this assessment; however, I cannot. Far from being the same routine each day, most days I spent deployed brought something different. I was involved in counseling, events, services, meetings, trips to the embassy; our chapel team was in constant motion due to the fact that we were the only chapel team at that location, and our team consisted of only two people. In all that I did, saw and experienced in the desert, nothing was more intriguing or unexpected than working with the Underground believers in the Kingdom.

Persecuted Christians have for centuries taken their faith and worship underground, sometimes literally but usually metaphorically. While they are not boisterous about their faith in public, privately they quietly and faithfully worship, serve God and share the truth of Jesus Christ wherever they might find themselves. They are far from being cowards; on the contrary, they are very brave, for it would be much easier to just get along without confessing Jesus Christ as Lord than it is to stay faithful in a region which rejects His truth. Such is the case in the Kingdom.

The Saudi Arabian government monitors the modes of communication of its people as well as our base, including emails and telephone conversations. A person in my position had to be very careful of what was said over the phone lines or through electronic messaging. One day I received a phone call that I had been expecting, although I did not know when it would come. The voice on the other end said, "Captain, the pick up and delivery is tonight…" He told me the time we would meet at the villa and he hung up. That was all the voice said, but it was all he needed to say. I understood exactly what was about to take place. The supplies in the villa would finally go to the intended location. That night I met the man behind the voice; he came with a non-descript delivery truck. As I helped him load the food and supplies, he explained the situation.

Most of the TCNs coming to Saudi Arabia on worker visas are men, but some are women. I found this odd because females of any nationality are forbidden to be in public alone; they must be with their husband or another male member of the family. They are also banned from driving, are not allowed to speak in public and are barred from most jobs; however, females can be employed as nurses, maids or nannies.

The shelter was located in the middle of Riyadh. The women secretly living there were former nannies or maids who had escaped abusive situations. Once any worker arrives in the Kingdom, their sponsor/employer confiscates their passport. After this happened, many found themselves in virtual slavery; the women at the shelter had been physically and many times sexually abused by their employer. There is no escape from this situation. They cannot go to the police; they had no civil rights. They cannot leave the country because they did not possess a passport and couldn't move freely in public anyway. So, many of those who find themselves in this inescapable situation either give up, live a life of abuse, or they commit suicide.

Complicating the situation further is the fact that some of the sexually assaulted women become pregnant by Saudi nationals. The general belief is that a faithful Saudi Muslim man would never engage in that type of deviant and sinful behavior; therefore, the woman must have committed fornication, which further lowers her status in society. While pregnant, the sponsoring person for whom she works is obligated to take care of her until the child is born; once the child is born, it is viewed as a Muslim child. No mother would ever leave her child behind in such an oppressive nation, even though some are given the opportunity to leave after the child is born; but they cannot take the child with them under any circumstances. The child is considered a Muslim and the mother is an infidel; infidels are not permitted to raise Muslim children.

In response to this situation, the underground Christian community, both Catholics and Protestants, began a battered women's shelter to help these women leave the country. This has proved to be very difficult because some of the women had been there as long as six or seven years. There is a small network of Christians, working directly with the women in the shelter and supplying it. To keep everyone safe, those working to supply the shelter ever met the other members of the network or even knew how many other people there actually were in existence. For a brief moment in time, I found myself as a part of a very secretive network of people.

On that particular night, nearly 5,000 pounds of food and supplies were delivered to 158 women and six children at the shelter. The only thing that worried me was the fact that if any one of the people involved got caught, things could turn really ugly, really fast. I was right. Several days after the midnight run, that same voice came across my cell phone once again, saying that he was on the way to the airport and was leaving the country and wouldn't be back. He gave no other explanation, and then hung up. I can only assume that he was caught and had been deported; but the work continues.

During my tour in the desert, I had the privilege of meeting two pastors involved in the underground church in Saudi Arabia; neither of whom ever met the other. Both had come as workers to the Kingdom and both worked in quiet, effective ways for the Kingdom of God. I remember going to prayer with each of them separately during the same week after a crackdown by the Mutawwa across the city against Christians. Neither was arrested or detained, but the whole situation of persecution brought a great sadness to my spirit, especially when I compared their fervency and faithfulness with that of American Christians.

As Americans, we live in such a privileged nation that we have grown complacent. In our country, our government protects our personal freedom of worship, and if we don't like our government, we change its leaders through the ballot box. We live in relative peace and safety. We can go anywhere we please at any time if we have the determination to do so. And yet, on Sunday morning, many find it so difficult to roll out of bed and go to worship at a local church; while on the other side of the globe, people who might lose their lives for worshipping at the Cross, intently seek out and find places and people who honor Christ. It struck me that the underground believers in KSA pray for the freedom every day that we take for granted, while ignoring God's grace in our lives.

In many ways, being in Saudi Arabia was similar to taking a step back in time, not only culturally, but also spiritually as well. For the first time in my life, I met men and women who truly knew what it was like to love God more than life itself; to live under the constant threat of persecution and to risk everything in the world for the one thing that ultimately matters the most.

When we read the Book of Acts in the Bible, we see a persecuted church, a faithful group of people sharing Christ's truth, and a unity brought by the Holy Spirit. The same can be said of the believers in KSA; I will admire them and their faithfulness to our Lord for the rest of my life. When I pray, I pray for them.

I cannot say on these pages all that I did or experienced with the underground; only that it was rewarding. The truth of it is that if too much is said or names are given, real lives might be placed in jeopardy; I fear that I may have said too much already. I can say that this experience made me a better person and pastor of my church. I can say that I was humbled and honored to have been among them; to have loved them and be loved by them; to have worshipped in their midst and to still serve the same Lord alongside of them. Most of all, while I may never see any of them again in this life, I truly look forward to that great day when we are reunited before the throne of Almighty God in His presence and His peace.

Chapter 6

Ray was Right

"When you go to get a haircut, be sure to go back home..." begins the chorus of a famous song by Ray Stevens. The tune covers a wide spectrum of events that can happen to you (all bad) when you go to an unfamiliar barber. After serving at Eskan Village, my assessment of his proclamations – Ray was absolutely right.

It wasn't long before I had to get my first haircut in the desert, but it has been my experience that not everyone who cuts hair has been created equal. My father had cut my hair in my younger years; learning the trade from my grandfather, who was a professional barber. During World War II, my grandfather cut hair on the side charging a quarter a head as he served with the 38th Infantry in the Pacific. I never paid for a haircut until basic training at Fort Knox in 1994. I am usually leery of going to new barbers, and it usually takes me several attempts in any location to find one who does the job to suit me. I didn't have much of an option in the desert; on base, there were only three barbers and one of those three was going to be the man who cut my hair.

But how hard could this be? I wear the simple "high and tight" military haircut. I was on an Air Force base. Each of the three men had been professionally trained and located at Eskan for years; I believed this was going to be the least of my problems while deployed. Looking back on it, I can't believe that I was so naïve.

All three barbers were Filipino, immediately presenting cultural and language barriers. Two were in one shop at the Breezeway; the third was located in a shop at the Base Exchange (BX). After sizing each of them up, I decided to go to the eldest of the three, believing he would have the most experience and would do a better job. Unknown to me was the fact that people in that part of the world are trained differently and do different things to accomplish the entire haircut experience.

I entered the shop and he pointed to the chair. The television in the shop was tuned in to Armed Forces Network and showing "CSI: Miami." I thought to myself, "This guy likes cop shows, he must be all right." Sitting down, he said, "How want it?" I told him I wanted a "high and tight," complete with hand gestures to simulate what I wanted on my head and speaking loud enough to drown out any other noises in the shop. I failed to realize that we had a language barrier, not a hard of hearing barrier.

He draped the cape over my body and began cutting away. As he began his mission, I noticed that he started at the top of the head, not on the sides like American barbers, but I didn't really care how he did it. A high and tight only takes a few minutes, no matter how you cut it. I had other places to be and other things to do; so, if this man wanted to start at the top and work his way down and around, it was fine by me because in less than 10 minutes, I should be on my way.

Thirty minutes later, he finally finished cutting my hair. He spun me around in the chair to face the mirror and said, "How look?" It looked just fine and I thought we were done, but it was at this point I made a critical, cultural error. I took my arms from under the cape, extended my hands and gave him a double "thumbs up" while saying, "fantastic, thank you." His expression totally changed; only then did I remember that giving someone a "thumbs up" in that region of the world is the equivalent of giving someone the middle finger in the United States. I had forgotten this very important detail.

The man grunted and unbeknownst to me began the second phase of every haircut in that part of the world; which I have come to call the 'lotion, oils and rub' phase, without which no haircut is complete. I had been warned of things like this in the past, but did not realize what it entailed.

The newly offended barber began squirting oil on my head, then taking cotton balls, he began to clean it as if he were cleaning a counter top;

slowly and methodically, but he wasn't gentle. I am quite certain through this whole process of the second phase, he was attempting to inflict pain on me. He succeeded.

After this oil or alcohol or whatever it was, he began to slap me with a towel like he was trying to buff the sides of my head as you would a pair of leather boots. All I could do was sit there and watch him hit me over and over with this towel, while in the mirror I could see my faithful assistant deriving great pleasure from this experience. Her joy was an endless stream of giggles.

Following this, he rubbed some type of lotion in his hands that smelled like dead flowers; then he started "massaging" my head. This man was so rough on my head I truly believed he was going to burn a hole in my scalp. After my head, he began rubbing my neck and shoulders; it was supposed to feel good, but it was more like a back-alley beat down.

When he was finally finished, forty-five minutes had passed since I first sat down and a breath of relief exited my body. I was so glad this was over. Following him to the cash register, he said, 'Twenty." To which I exclaimed, "Twenty dollars? For one haircut? It's higher here than in America." Through gritted teeth and a glare that would have undoubtedly killed a lesser man, he said, "Twenty *Riyals*, only five dollars." While this made much more sense, I had just offended this man a second time inside of an hour; therefore, I handed him a ten and walked out of the shop. I vowed that I would never put myself through that tormenting experience from him again. Afterward, my body ached for three days.

The second time I went for a haircut it would be different, very different. I went to the man at the BX; I had seen him around a few times and he was always friendly and always wore colorful shirts; purple seemed to be his favorite color along with a light green my assistant referred to as "lime." This in itself is what most detectives would call a clue.

I sat in this man's chair and he began cutting just like the other barber, but his shop was vastly different. On the wall were pictures of strikingly good-looking men sporting stylish haircuts. The television was tuned to professional wrestling, which he watched while cutting hair. During the haircut, this friendly, colorfully clad, young barber made a comment about how the wrestling tights of one of the men fit his lower body so nicely. This was another clue.

As I watched him work in the mirror, this barber did not venture to turn the swivel chair. Instead, he preferred to dance around the chair while he worked as if he was in a ballet. This was my final clue that allowed me to put it altogether. I am certain this man would have fit nicely in a hair salon or a beauty shop, for I am convinced he was gay. The bad thing was my assistant already knew this fact but had strongly recommended him on the advice of others just to torture me.

When it came to the second phase of the experience, this barber's lotion and oils were pink. That didn't bother me near as much as when he began rubbing my head, neck and shoulders. It may have just been in my head, but I am fairly certain when he began doing this, he was flirting with me. As my assistant and I walked out of that barbershop, she was quite gleeful about the experience. I turned to her and said, "That's two down, only one to go.

Several weeks later, I found myself in the chair of the third barber. When he asked me how I wanted it, I kept my hands down and said, "High and tight, you know, just shave it." Again, I had made yet another mistake. Before I could speak, I saw a flash go through the air as the man took a straight razor to my scalp and lopped off a chunk of hair. As it fell to the floor he said, "Like that?" I thought, "No, not like that..." but the damage was done and there was no way I could glue hair back on my head, so I told him that was fine and he proceeded to finish the job. It was my own fault anyway for being so stupid as to use the word "shave" in a sentence, knowing that TCNs take very literal every word you speak.

When I walked out of that shop, for the first time in my life I was completely bald; bearing a remarkable resemblance to Elmer Fudd. I even had more hair on my head on the day I was born. For the next two weeks I let no one take my picture at any time. I did discover something very important about those oils and lotions: they had to have been alcohol based because when he slapped them on my head it felt as if I had just stuck my head into a fire pit. Once again, this brought my assistant great joy and laughter.

In the end, I went back to the first barber; the man I had offended the very first time I received a haircut in the desert. By the time I returned, he did not remember me and once again he did a fantastic job – except I never used hand signals when communicating with him after the first fiasco. I stayed with him until the end of the tour; however, my haircut experience did make me appreciate even more the individual who cuts my hair back home. I affectionately refer to my "barber" as the "Hair goddess" as a running joke. She is heterosexual, doesn't watch TV while cutting hair, has never put me in a death grip, speaks English very well and sings in our church choir; these are qualities you just don't find everywhere you go. And I have now decided that if I am ever deployed to that region of the world, I will write to my wife and have her find a way to place this person in a footlocker and have it shipped to me overseas.

My haircut experiences from Eskan are humorous, and some of my cohorts in the desert had a lot of fun at my expense because of my trials and errors in this area. But at the same time some outstanding ministry was taking place as God opened hearts to His truth, took the blinders away from searching eyes to reveal Himself, and steered minds toward His Son. We often forget that it matters not what a person wears, what color or gender they might be, nor if their hair is all jacked out of place. What really matters is if they know Christ and if they are willing to be used by Him in His service. At Eskan Village, God was using me and I knew it and the reason I knew it is because people were coming to know Jesus Christ as their Lord.

Chapter 7

Confirmation

"Sir, they're on their way here right now. They will be here tomorrow night." It was an answer given to the commander by a Master Sergeant in our weekly Commander's Call for all senior enlisted personnel and officers. As we heard these words, I had no idea what the man was talking about; it sounded as if the bad guys were coming and we needed to lock and load. That idea changed when he clicked the slide on his presentation; the Miami Dolphin Cheerleaders were coming to Eskan Village as a part of the USO tour.

Man can only see a small, limited piece of God's great plan for our lives at any given time; such was the case with me when the cheerleaders arrived. I could only see a USO tour event to boost morale; in reality, this even was the first in a series of events that made possible a spiritual renewal at Eskan Village. At first glance, each of the events, situations and relationships that were forged during this time seem to be unconnected; however, in the grand scheme of what God was doing through His Holy Spirit, not only were these events connected, they were placed strategically by the hand of the lord so that He would be honored and gloried through our ministry in Saudi Arabia.

Chaplain Jack with Miami Dolphin Cheerleaders

I was in the DFAC when they arrived, sitting with LTC Wagner and some of his men. The cheerleaders went through the chow line and then fanned out among the troops; several sat at our table. Their sole purpose was to boost morale; the next evening they would perform a show similar to what they do at Miami's football games. During their visit, they signed autographs and visited with many of the troops; some even took pictures with them. A picture was taken of me with the cheerleaders; I am standing surrounded by four of them, all with big smiles on our faces. But that picture doesn't tell the whole story.

When the cheerleaders asked what our jobs were in the Air Force, they were surprised to find out that I was a chaplain; they had expected someone much older. It perked some of their interests because several of them were students at a Bible college in Florida. LTC Wagner began to describe the risky nature of my job in the Kingdom, talking about what might happen if I was ever get caught by the Mutawwa. He even went so far as to say that I had the "most dangerous job in Saudi Arabia." While I never thought of my position in that manner, there was some truth in what He had said because I was the only man on base with a price on my head.

As the conversation moved forward, I asked some of them if they would go to the chapel office with me. In the chapel office, we had a common area with 24/7 access to moral phones and wireless internet for personal laptops. Sometimes I would have airmen become hermits using the internet and rarely coming out to socialize, but I figured they needed a lift in morale as well. The cheerleaders complied.

Before they left that evening to go to another part of the base, the cheerleader coach asked me if I could write them a team prayer to be used before games and performances. I went back to the office and spent about 45 minutes wording a concise prayer that would fit their circumstance. It reads:

"Almighty God, Thank you for the talents and gifts you have given us, and for the opportunity to use them. As we perform today, we pray we will use our abilities to bring joy and entertainment in the lives of others. Together, we ask that you will direct our path, protect us from harm and guide us into that which is good. In your name we pray, Amen."

Later that evening I found the cheerleader coach and handed her the prayer, she read it and said that they would use it the next day and the following season. She also told me that they would put it up in their section of the Miami Dolphin history museum. When I returned stateside, I received a manila envelope from the Dolphins; it contained a letter thanking me and a picture of the prayer I had written and the background was of the cheerleading squad at one of their home games. This one simple prayer has now become the official performance prayer of the Miami Dolphin Cheerleaders.

A few days later, I learned that I was being watched that night. Some of the airmen wanted to see if the young chaplain really practiced what he preached. I must have passed their test because I led one of them to Christ just a few weeks later and baptized him in theatre.

About this same time God moved unexpectedly through a ministry loss. Eskan's long-time Friday school teacher was leaving due to retirement. Loraine was a civilian DoD contractor who truly loved the Lord and the people. She had spent years of service to the Lord in Saudi Arabia, and we decided to make her last service at the Breezeway a memorable one. She received gifts and cards, but I didn't know what I should give her; so, I did the only thing I knew she would absolutely appreciate. At the end of the service, I called her down front, thanked her for her service and called on anyone who would to come forward and lay hands on her in prayer as she prepared to go home. When it was over, she was absolutely elated, just as thrilled as if I had just given her a million dollars. She went on and on to the whole congregation how blessed she felt and then she said, "…and from a white preacher, who would have ever thought that?"

Everyone laughed at that, and it was funny in a way, but also sad in another. Loraine had grown up in the Deep South during segregation. As Jim Crowe died a slow death, I am certain she endured the pains of discrimination; pains which are still in her memory today. Yet, on that day, as God was moving within us and among us, we were all of one race (human) and one people (God's). Through this ministry loss, all of us, white, black, Hispanic, Filipino and others, were given a wonderful gift – racial barriers came down and we became color blind.

Loraine was a good lady and I hated to lose her. A few months later I did get a chance to talk to her on Easter Friday via the phone. I told her of the baptisms and salvations that had taken place, and she was thrilled and spoke words of encouragement. She was also sad because she couldn't be there to witness it. I'm looking forward to the day I see this Saint of God again.

In a chaplaincy ministry, relationships are essential; relationships are what makes the ministry effective. Over the course of time, I was able to form solid relationships with two groups of people that affected the ministry in the desert. The first group were the men from the Explosive Ordinance Disposal shop – EOD for short; the other was with the other officers on base. These groups were strikingly different, but both were very good at what they did.

There were only four men of EOD, all enlisted. EOD is a small career field because they work with bombs for a living; they find bombs, disarm the device or blow it up. These men were extremely intelligent and often challenged me in deep theological questions when I visited their shop. Sometimes we'd talk for hours; at other times we'd play cards; and once they even showed me how to build an explosive – for training purposes only, of course. One day they let me blow up a refrigerator in the desert; that isn't something a person gets to do every day. Each time I was with them, regardless of what we did together, we were forming a bond, and eventually I baptized one of them.

The other group was the officers. One night after a going away reception for one of the females who worked in the DFAC, Captain

Kevin Green, the logistics officer, came up to me and asked what I was doing that night. I said, "Kevin, I'm sorry, but I'm a married man." He laughed, not expecting that remark, and told me that the staff officers got together every Saturday night to watch a movie and was inviting me to join with them. Evidently they had talked it over amongst themselves and decided I might be a good addition to the group. There was only one problem – he said it was at "Skeet's" place. I thought, "Who the heck is Skeet?"

Skeet was the call name of our lone pilot on base. His job was to monitor all air traffic coming into or out of Saudi Arabia. When I showed up, I hardly knew the others even though there were only seven of us. There were no commanders and no enlisted there – just us. To my surprise, those nights turned out to be the most relaxing of the entire tour. Of this group, including myself, five of the seven were believers; including one female, 1LT Kate Lockhart. I became close to three men in this group: Major Dave Balda, Captain Victor Lewis and Green. All three of them were Christians, and all three of them are really good officers and a credit to the United States Air Force.

The most important result of forming the relationships I had with these people, both the officers and EOD, was the fact that *the chaplain* was being accepted as part of their groups. This is very difficult to do on an American base and even more so in a deployed location. Often a chaplain or minister is seen as an outsider who can't really fit in anywhere, but this wasn't the case at Eskan. As it turned out, God not only reached some through me in these groups, but He also used them to help me become a better minister and a better officer in the Air Force.

January and February had passed; March was underway and would bring to Saudi Arabia the largest dust storm in 30 years. The pictures of it rolling in looked like something out of "*The Ten Commandments*," and when it hit, all I could see was orange. The dust was everywhere and in everything. The morning after it was over, I walked out to see my formerly white car, which had set out in the storm, now a nice shade of brown. I hired a man for about $6 a week to wash the car inside and out; he earned his pay that week.

Dust Storm

The month of March also brought a softball league to the troops, giving me yet another opportunity to be among more people. With some of the night shift 130th AW people, we formed the "Mostly Mountaineers" because most of us were from West Virginia. Of all sports I have played throughout the years, I was always best at baseball; softball would be no different.

It has been said that God moves in mysterious ways. I have found this to be true. I believed that softball would bring our chapel team to more ministry effectiveness. This did happen, but not the way I had planned. I thought God would move in hearts and minds because of our witness and activity during the softball season. As it turned out, God moved in hearts and minds through my inactivity due to a injury while playing softball.

I was looking forward to playing all season; late night practices on a field that was solid sand with no grass, but containing a few rocks mixed in for good measure. It was like playing on sand paper. In our first game we lost by a large margin. During that game, I was running from first to second base and felt a "pop" in the back of my right leg and went down immediately. My teammates carried me off the field and straight to the base clinic.

The doctor in the clinic was a TCN, but a doctor nonetheless. I was in so much pain that he couldn't examine me. He told the nurse to give me a shot of morphine. It began taking effect within 15 minutes, but I was still in pain; the only difference was that I was now drugged. He couldn't examine me well, so he told me to go to the villa and come back in the morning. He gave me two morphine tablets just in case I needed them; which was rare because narcotics, even for medical purposes, are extremely difficult to come by in Saudi Arabia. In my morphine-induced stupor, I said, "But doctor, how am I going to take a shower?" He was silent, so I began making eye contact with every person in the room; most of whom were just smiling at me. My eyes finally found my assistant, TSgt Claudette Arms, who looked me squarely in the eyes and said, "That just isn't in my job description."

The next day I hobbled back into the doctor's office on crutches. He believed that it was only a strained muscle and gave me a handful of muscle relaxers and Motrin for the pain. It would be ten days later before I could finally convinced them to send me to the hospital in downtown Riyadh for an MRI.

The hospital was an amazing sight. The architecture was gorgeous and seemed to be a collision of the modern and ancient worlds. Instead of tile, they had solid marble floors. There were several levels to the hospital with an elevator, but was seldom used it. Most people opted for the marble, spiral staircase with the solid brass railings. All the nurses were Filipino but the surgeon who performed and read the MRI was a Saudi. After the MRI, he sat me down and said, "My practice is in Chicago. I only come here about two months out of the year and work. Even if we were in America, I would not recommend surgery." He told me that the muscle was torn, but in time it would heal just as good as if he repaired it and the recovery time would be about the same. Ultimately, he left the surgery decision up to me; I opted not to forgo the surgery.

My mobility was restricted during this time, and I knew I couldn't continue ministry as I had been doing it. But by this time I had already established myself. Then two things happened that I wasn't expecting. The first was the fact that the people I had been witnessing to and praying for began accepting Christ. The second amazing thing was that there was a small group of women who ministered to me.

There had been several men and women asking questions about the faith; they were hungry for answers. It wasn't until I was injured that the majority of the people I led to Christ actually accepted Him as Savior.

There were others who had made a confession, but had never been baptized; there were also some who wanted to rededicate their life to Jesus. As each one came to me privately, and then to Christ publicly, I saw a different chapter to an age long tale. Each personal story was different, but all shared a common theme – emptiness in the heart and that this was now the time to make a decision and come home. Each time, I felt so humbled at what was taking place and to have been a part of their decision. Several said it was my teaching that pushed them over the edge to make the decision; but it wasn't me at all, it was God's Holy Spirit using me for His glory. The thought of being used in this way by God is very special and if that doesn't bring humility to a man, that person has a heart made of stone and a soul that suffers from spiritual anemia.

Being immobilized was frustrating, but Claudette shined as a true servant during this time. Had it not been for her tireless work, our ministry would not have been as effective. In fact, she was so impressive that I did the paperwork to make sure that she would be recognized for all she did in the desert. When we returned to our home base, she received that recognition, being awarded the Air Force Achievement Medal. Without question, she had earned it.

Claudette did more than just ministry work for our chapel team; she along with three other women ministered to me during this time period. Along with Claudette, TSgt Lora Schemeltz, TSgt Tonya Cabellero, and SSgt Jen Kane, all with different faith backgrounds and unique personalities, but all ministered to me.

The morning after I was injured, the pain was so bad that I couldn't sleep. I hobbled on my crutches over to the DFAC at about 0430. The TCN chefs took great pity on me and brought me a huge breakfast and a cup of coffee, and I was thankful for that. I sat in the DFAC until 0900 waiting for the doctor to arrive in his office. During that four and half hour period, every person on base came through that building, and every one of them asked me about the injury. I decided that for things to go smoothly, I would go very early to the DFAC to eat or just before it closed, or I would just eat something in the villa and stay out of everybody's way. These women weren't going to let that happen. Every day, three times a day for three weeks, one or usually all of these ladies escorted me to the DFAC and served me chow – and a lot of it. I don't think they realized how much I truly appreciated all that they did for me.

The injury was in the back of my right thigh and it was a fairly severe tear. It hurt to sit in a normal position, but a recliner in my villa took the pressure off my leg. Soon, I found myself staying in that recliner most of the time. Lora decided that it wasn't good for me to do that, so she found another recliner on base and had it set up in the chapel office. That was a really nice gesture.

Jen was a Roman Catholic and a solid believer. Sometimes we clashed intellectually because of our different faith traditions, but pure hearts always make up for strong opinions. This was her last deployment; she had decided to leave the Air Force and enter the convent in her quest to become a nun. I have no doubt that this was a true calling on her life. She was at nearly every service, both Protestant and Catholic, showing she had a hungry heart for Christ's truth. As the tour drew to an end, Claudette would leave Saudi before I did because our replacements had not yet arrived. In that period of time, Jen basically functioned as my assistant and performed wonderfully. Chaplain Bergbower, our visiting Catholic Chaplain from the 379th, once referred to her as "a woman with no guile in her heart." Without equivocation, he was right.

Tonya was a joyful, bubbly lady from the African-American Baptist tradition, and a true joy to be around and to have known. Her care and concern for people was evident. As the softball season was winding down, I decided I was healed enough to give it a try once again, and I did OK. But these four women didn't like it one bit. Tonya 'dropped a dime' to my wife through email, asking her to tell me to quit doing things that might re-injure my leg. I have never been one to mistake my rank with my wife's authority; thus, my illustrious softball career ended in the desert, but my appreciation for these women who cared from me at Eskan only grew.

One tragedy of American Christianity in our time is the fact we have lost a solid, Biblical teaching with regards to the doctrine of suffering. We have forgotten that Christians will sometimes go through trials, tribulations and dark times for the sake of the Kingdom. In those times, we ask why these things happen to us; forgetting that faith is a lot like film – it has to be in the dark to be developed. Pain and suffering is not always caused by a lack of faith or sin. Sometimes God has ordained our suffering for reasons we do not always understand in the moment of suffering. Yet, if God has ordained our suffering and placed us in that position, the most faithful thing we can do is to accept it, learn from it and grow in Him while it is taking place. It did not make sense to me what God was doing at the time of the injury, but God would later reveal what He was doing. Through this injury God had largely immobilized me, which made me available privately for anyone who wished to come and ask deep spiritual questions that were plaguing their lives. During my time of suffering, God was opening hearts, minds and doors so that the lost could enter His Kingdom by faith.

All of these things separately do not seem like much; but when they are put together the truth is that ministry was happening at Eskan. I kept preaching and teaching just as I always had; but now solid relationships were formed that stretched throughout the base. When I was immobilized, people didn't feel like they were interrupting me or bothering me – so they'd drop by and see how I was doing and ask questions they had on their hearts. Things were coming together doing ministry throughout the Chapel community because I needed help. As a result people were coming to Christ. It was a confirmation of what I had prayed for, hoped for and wanted more than anything. By April, all the pieces were in place, God made it happen as He brought us together and He was glorified in the Kingdom.

Chapter 8

April Awakening

"Difficult to determine if *any* will be saved or baptized. Too early to tell; have to wait and see." So began the words written in my journal a few days after arriving in the Kingdom. At the time, I believed the outlook was bleak, but what I found were hearts hungry for the Gospel and souls soaking up the Word of God like a sponge.

The one constant in the ministry throughout the years at Eskan had been the music. Over time, the musicians had changed, singers had come and gone, instruments floated in and out, but the actual music at the chapel services was outstanding. Any time you have men and women dedicated to the music ministry at this level of quality and at the same time you have solid teaching to accompany it, God can do great things through willing vessels – and that's exactly what He did in the desert.

I had geared all services to compliment one another in two phases. The first would climax at Easter and the second would close my ministry at Eskan as I was replaced by the next rotation's chaplain. It made perfect sense because after Easter I would be on the downhill slide toward heading home. What I had not expected in the midst of my planning was a DV visit from Chaplain Colonel Bristol, the AFCENT Command Chaplain. This was to take place during Easter weekend. Part of the Command

Chaplain's job was to go to every base in theatre and visit the chaplain at that particular base for support, encouragement and guidance. While this visit was appreciated, in the back of my mind I believed that it could not have come at a worse or more stressful time.

When a DV visits, the hosting party, which was me, is supposed to give tours of the base, prepare the accommodations, take the DV around the base for various demonstrations given by different shops, meet the commanders, take part in the daily routine, and without question, host a DV dinner where all the top officers and enlisted personnel are invited to attend. This is standard protocol; however, knowing how God had been moving up to that point and knowing our plans for Easter, I knew that this DV visit was not going to follow standard protocol, for I was not going to quench the Spirit.

Throughout February and March, an amazing thirteen men and women confessed Jesus Christ as their Savior and eleven of them wanted to make a public profession of faith through baptism. It seemed only appropriate to have this take place on Easter. In the Kingdom, Easter was not celebrated on Sunday morning as it is in America; it is celebrated on what they called Easter Friday, which is Good Friday in the western world. There would be a sunrise service on Easter Sunday, but most people worked because it was a regular workday in the Kingdom; everyone had a day off on Friday. Therefore, on Easter Friday in the Kingdom, eleven new believers in Jesus Christ would be baptized regardless of the Distinguished Visitors that were coming.

After making the plans, I was informed that Chaplain Bristol and his assistant, SMSgt Benningfield, would arrive on the Thursday before Easter Friday. By this time, I had read past itineraries of previous chaplains in the continuity binder and I had spoken with Major Balda for direction on this matter. I knew what I was supposed to do. I also knew that I couldn't accomplish the task of the DV visit as it was normally done and honor Christ through the baptisms while making a trip to the Embassy for Easter Friday services all at the same time. I decided to take the DV plans on base a different route, but to make it all work together and work right, I needed a lot of help from my chapel community.

Two weeks before Easter Friday, I stood before my congregation at the Breezeway and explained my situation. General Van Sickle was allowing us to use the pool behind his villa for the baptisms; I was thankful for that because it was the only place on base with actual grass and trees. Using that area meant that we would be adjacent to the villa occupied by Rick and Nancy Jackson; this was a fairly uncommon privilege, but it would serve our purposes nicely. Prior to this, some had talked of an Easter fellowship after the baptisms, so, on that morning, I put it all together in one package.

I told them that after the services in the morning, I would have to go to the Embassy. At 1630 I would be back on base and we would gather and gather for the baptisms. Instead of a DV dinner where we would all have to rush to make it, I decided that we could turn it into an entire evening of fellowship. My thought process was the fact that my first responsibility as a chaplain was to honor and glorify God; my second responsibility was to take care of my people. If I was to err, I would err on the side of the people who had been entrusted to my care in the desert.

The people were thrilled and worked on this event for two weeks. They planned and bought food for a cookout, designed games with Easter themes and a lot of people worked together to pull it off. There had never been anything like this before, but we were certain this would be a great night.

When Chaplain Bristol arrived, we gave him the customary tour of the base, presented a slide show of our work on base, talked about the ministry, and made the commander call to Colonel Hatcher; all of it went well. On Easter Friday, the services went very well and we were told that our services were "more like a church service rather than a chapel." I was glad to hear that because that had been my goal from Day One.

After returning from the Embassy, it was time to meet for the baptisms. Claudette and I stepped into the pool – it would be the first time a female had ever assisted me in a baptism and it was the first time she had ever taken part in a baptism other than her own. The first to profess his faith and be baptized was the first man I had led to Christ in the desert, Senior Airman Robert Chaney, who worked in EOD. He had walked by the chapel tent one day and heard people playing the instruments and it sounded really good. He later came to me and asked if he could use the instruments. One day he was playing and got roped into playing with the band, stayed for the service, and kept coming; he also began asking questions about faith and the meaning of baptism. I wasn't long afterwards that he accepted Jesus as his personal Savior. After he was saved, he shared his new faith with his young wife over the phone; once he returned home he promised to find a church family where his family would be able to learn and grow in the Lord.

Baptism of SrA Robert Chaney

The second person I baptized was a Filipino lady who was a wife of one of the civilian contractors; both became very special people to me and Claudette while in the desert. She had been raised a Roman Catholic, but after marriage began attending Protestant services with her husband wherever they had worked. While I was injured, both came to see me in the chapel office, and it was there that she accepted Christ by faith.

One by one they entered the pool behind the general's house. One by one they professed their faith in Christ and went under the water to be symbolically raised in the newness of life. In all, eleven men and women were baptized. Some were white, some were black, others were of Asian descent. Some of them converted from other faiths; some had no faith or religious preference prior to accepting Christ. I baptized people who originally came from America, Nigeria and the Philippines; I even had the privilege of baptizing a Choctaw Indian. Only later did I learn from Chaplain Bristol that at that moment, God had just allowed me to baptize more people on that day than any other chaplain in the history of Eskan Village Air Base and more people than any other chaplain during that rotation. But in all of it, only God can be praised; for it is Him and Him alone who calls the sinner to salvation by faith through His grace.

Baptism group picture

The celebration afterwards was fantastic. Rick and Nancy were always wonderful hosts and they truly love the Lord. It was a joyous night, but deep inside me something was missing. On the other side of the planet, the other half of me, the half of me that holds my heart, was at home with our children. Nancy asked me how the evening was going and I told her everything was wonderful and that she had done wonders in making it a beautiful night; even Chaplain Bristol was impressed. I said that everything was indeed wonderful except for one thing. The only thing that could have made it perfect was if my wife Tina could have been there. She fully understood my feelings. While I was joyous over what God had done at Eskan, on another level I was very lonely.

Saturday morning dawned and we had our last meeting with Chaplain Bristol and SMSgt Benningfield. The one reward an airman receives for doing a good job is a commander's coin; and both Claudette and I received Chaplain Bristol's coin. When he shook my hand he said we were an "impressive team who has performed beyond all expectations." I saluted and thanked him, and with that he was on his way back to his home base, some 800 miles away. As of that moment, I could breathe a sigh of relief and prepare for the Sunrise Service on Easter morning at the Oasis of Peace Chapel.

On Easter morning, people in the United States awoke to the news that an American citizen had been rescued by the Navy at sea after being hijacked and held for days by Somalia pirates/terrorists. That entire operation took place as the sun rose over the Kingdom. As I watched the sky, a rare thing was happening – clouds dotted the atmosphere. On that morning, God splashed across the Saudi sky a brilliance of color; reminding all that our Creator is still creative in His handiwork.

Due to the schedules of those in the chapel community who worked for the permanent party side of base, the service could be a maximum of 45 minutes beginning at 0630. Just two days before, I had experienced the greatest day of ministry in my life; but on this day, on Easter morning, I watched as only a handful of regulars began to enter. It was a depressing shot to the heart and soul. As the music began for the opening song, only 18 people were in the chapel.

My eyes were focused on the band. I couldn't bear to look at many people. Standing up front, I felt a few come and sit behind me, but I believed it was going to be a low crowd. When the band finished, I turned to welcome the congregation and I couldn't believe what I was seeing. The chapel had gone from a handful of worshippers to standing room only; the people were packed wall to wall. There were Catholics and Protestants, officers and enlisted; various races, colors and nationalities were in this tent. At first, I was so overwhelmed I could barely speak, then a shaft of light went through my soul at that moment. Standing before them, God spoke to me; not in an audible voice, it was much louder than that – I now understood why I was called to Eskan. In that moment I knew that I was created for that place, that time, that country and that people. For that one moment in time, there was no question nor equivocation, I knew that I was perfectly in the will and plan of God for my life and the lives of every person I had come in contact with in the Kingdom. When a man realizes this fact about himself, it is humbling but also very powerful because only then does one know that you are truly an instrument being used by Almighty God for His glory.

That morning, I preached Christ exclusively as the Savior, Redeemer and Lord of us all. Throughout the service there were people saying 'amen' and raising hands praising Him. Without question, not only was that the most powerful and meaningful service I performed at Eskan Village; it was the most powerful Easter service I have ever experienced in my entire life.

Afterwards, I shook every hand and hugged every person that would receive a hug. We were one in the bonds of Christ and we all knew that something very special had taken place over the last 72 hours. As I thought back to the baptisms, the leading people to salvation in Christ, the service we had just experienced and the joy and love we all shared, I knew it was a glimpse of what the eternal Kingdom of God will be like. There were no racial boundaries, no boundaries of enlisted or officer, no walls of religious tradition; there was only Jesus Christ. And that is exactly how heaven is described; all of the King's children praising Him for eternity. It is for this reason that this one service at Eskan Village is still the most meaningful day of ministry I have ever taken part in or experienced; we were one in the Spirit of God's Holy Son.

As we left the chapel, the mid-morning prayer of the Muslims came over the nationwide PA system. We had all heard their calls to prayer every day, five times a day. As I listened, I thought to myself, "We might be in the Kingdom of Islam's two most sacred sites of Mecca and Medina; but we have just given them one huge shot in the jaw for the good guys."

Chapter 9

Morale Trip

Easter celebrations lasted three days at Eskan Village and culminated with the the Commander giving the troops a half-day off and the officers serving the meals in the chow line at the DFAC. I had never seen officers do this for the men and women serving under them, but it was an excellent gesture. The meal that was served was absolutely fantastic; it was a traditional Easter meal and for the first time in many months, we were able to consume ham. Pork products are illegal in the Kingdom, so this made it extra special. In America just about everyone eats ham several times a week; but to us, it was a huge event. In fact, many people took pictures of the Easter spread.

Easter was over and Claudette and I had to begin preparing ourselves and our positions for our replacements. We knew we would build continuity books, which are instruction booklets of what you do to make the transition easier for the next person occupying the position. We knew we had to start preparing our chapel community for the transition, and we knew we had to begin mentally preparing for our departure from wartime active duty airmen to peacetime civilians.

Before any of that took place, we were allotted one day of authorized off-base activity in the desert, the coveted reward of a morale trip. The 64th

AEG jointly with the permanent party contingency of USMTM had began a program a couple of months earlier where a permanent party member could, if approved, invite the airmen on rotation off base for dinner, shopping, site seeing, golfing, or whatever they decided to do. The couple who invited Claudette and me had chosen to do it all and make an entire day of the morale trip. Our hosts were a married couple; I had baptized the female and her husband was a civilian defense contractor. Both had spent years in that region of the world, and were very knowledgeable about the language and culture. I realized how savvy they were when I learned that they had scheduled all of our activities around the daily calls to prayer.

TSgt Arms in Arabic Dress

Natives of that region plan their day around the heat of the desert and the calls to prayer. Many places close down from noon to four o'clock, deeming it too hot to do business. They then reopen and stay open until nearly eleven at night. They also close down for the time periods when the call to prayer takes place. The reason is because it is illegal to operate businesses when the prayer time is going on. To enforce this law, the Mutawwa patrol the streets making sure people are where they are supposed to be and business doors are locked. If customers were inside a business or restaurant when the initial prayer call sounded, that was OK, but the doors were locked and no one could get in or out.

We left at eight in the morning, I was wearing civilian clothes and Claudette had on her traditional abaya without a veil, which we had learned was acceptable for American women. The first place we stopped was a souk, this was a new concept for me. A souk is basically an open flea market with structures for the shops and the merchandise is high quality. There were various souks throughout the city, but this one and the shop we entered was familiar to my host. It was a Persian rug shop with rugs made by the owner, who was Persian; my host had done much business with him in the past and knew many of the other shop owners. I felt pretty good about this situation, mainly because he had been acquainted with this man for several years.

After our introductions, the man made small talk with us and our host, but then he asked the most fearful question any Muslim could have asked me in open public forum. He simply said, "And what do you do?" I previously wondered what I would say if I was ever asked this question, knowing there was a price on my head by the Mutawwa. I said, "Well, I'm in the Air Force." The man smiled and said, "I know, but what do you do on base?" I wasn't sure what to say, but before any words formed in my mouth, my host said, "He is our pastor on base." I was told never to tell anyone off-base what my position was, and my host had just blown my cover. Claudette and I looked at each other and I was certain that I had just broken teeth as my jaw hit the ground.

The man fully understood what being a pastor meant. It meant I was a leader of Christians. It meant I wanted everybody to be a Christian. It also meant a hefty reward for a cash-deprived person. To me, it meant instant fear.

The Persian man's expression changed, but then he did something unexpected. He went into the next room and brought out the best chair in the shop, *his* chair. Asking me to sit down and rest, my host nodded to me; so, I did as I was asked. I felt odd, not knowing what he was doing, and then he asked us all to just wait a few minutes. He took off out the door and ran down the alley; in my mind I was thinking he had gone to retrieve the Mutawwa and I was about to become a martyr for the faith. Yet, my host was not worried one bit.

When the man returned he brought with him freshly baked breakfast bread and a hot tea of sorts on a silver platter. He served me first, then Claudette (thinking she was my wife), and then the others. The bread had been freshly baked just minutes earlier by his wife, in a stone oven, which is why he had run down the alley. He had wanted to retrieve it while it was still hot and fresh out of the oven. He served the tea in the same sequence as the bread; with it, he provided me and only me, with real sugar, an honor in his culture because real sugar was not always readily available. Most sweeteners are in liquid form. Both the tea and the bread were absolutely delicious and he waited on me as his honored guest.

After we left, I asked my host about this unexpected and unusual experience. He told me that to the average Muslim, the main issue was not whether you were a Christian or followed Islam, but that you are a monotheist. The man had recognized me as a leader of a monotheistic faith, serving only one God. While he believed I was erring in my worship of the One True God, it was his belief (and the belief of most average Muslims) that I was trying to serve Him the best way I knew how. In his rationale, he believed he should honor me as he would a religious leader of Islam, thereby pleasing Allah.

As the sun grew in strength, we visited various shops and saw many people out and about doing exactly what Americans would do in a shopping mall. They shopped, talked and roamed from place to place looking for the best prices. Some in were large families, others were in small groups of men and occasionally you would see a group of women together, mostly at the shops catering to women. Their shops contained different products than American stores, but that is to be expected because the culture calls for different items.

A Saudi woman is covered from head to toe in all black, but it amazed me how many shops there were that contained nothing but these black outfits. The women in the shops would go through 30 or 40 of these robe-like outfits, trying to pick out the one they wanted. I mean, seriously... they were all the *same*, how long could it possibly take to choose a black robe with a matching black veil? The funny thing was that their husbands would wait outside on a bench for them to pick one and buy it, all the while shaking their heads wondering what was taking so long, just like an American man waiting for his wife in a dress shop.

At one souk, I saw two women shopping together – and an amazing thing happened, something that will probably never happen to me ever again. I was in close proximity to these two women, who wore veils; indicating that they were Saudi women. They were softly talking and occasionally, they would glance at me. I had grown a mustache to blend in with the cultural norms; I also had a very dark tan, so dark that many people who did not know me would automatically begin speaking Arabic, thinking I was a Saudi. I watched these two women the best I could without making eye contact; eye contact with a woman who is not a relative is thought to be a dishonor in their culture. After a few minutes of trying to make out what they were saying to each other, and watching them glance over at me, I decided the next time they did this I was going to look them squarely in the eyes. When I did this, I could tell that they were smiling behind those veils; I could see it in their eyes. At this time, much to my surprise, both of these women removed their veils and showed me their faces. This happened very quickly, for in that culture it is illegal and dishonorable to show anyone your face except your husband or close family members.

In that quick moment, the sheer natural beauty of these two women struck me. I had been in the desert four months at that point and I truly missed my wife, but these women were not the type of attractive you observe after four months in the desert – they were truly naturally beautiful. Seeing a Saudi female face dumbfounded me; I was stunned. Later, I asked my host about what had happened and he laughed harder than I had seen a man laugh for quite a while. He said that it was very rare for that to happen; the women only do it for a specific purpose. If the man told what they did, it would dishonor their family. In short, my host just informed me that those two women were making a proposal of marriage; it is a very rare and very forward way of saying that they were available and willing to be my wife instantly. This is not unusual in Saudi because a man can have up to four wives. While it was an ego boost to have these women find me worthy of being their 'shared' husband, somehow I do not think my wife Tina would have approved if I returned home with two new brides in tow.

After leaving the souks, we stopped by the infamous place we affectionately called "Chop, Chop Square." Here, the executions of criminals and newly converted Christians were held every Friday. It was built similar to an outdoor stadium in the shape of a huge square with an open roof. As we passed through the archways to enter the actual square, I noticed that they had vending machines with refreshments available for those who came to watch the public executions. These machines were well-used, for the executions draw thousands every Friday. We didn't stay there long because the Mutawwa is housed in that building and I did not want to be their next star attraction.

As the day wore on and I interacted with the people, I began to understand their culture much better. In just a few hours, I began to function as they function in their society, a concept which is nearly unknown in America. We do not expect immigrants or visitors from other countries to blend in and become part of our 'melting pot' anymore. Instead, we believe in the absurd idea that we can accommodate every one and every culture. Instead of being a 'melting pot' we've become more like a fruit salad; all maintaining their own culture and being thrown into one big bowl. In truth, I believe the Saudis have a better grip and understanding on this issue than Americans.

On one street there were various shops set up in a department store fashion that America had in earlier decades. Each of these shops had a distinct national/cultural ownership. For example, the Filipinos ran the meat/fish market; the Lebanese maintained the bakeries and sweet shops, and so forth. This was very interesting because each culture brought its own flavor to the market place, while still observing the norms of society. It was in this quarter of Riyadh where I can face-to-face with the most dreaded and feared men in Saudi Arabia – the Mutawwa.

Walking down the sidewalk, I noticed a man dressed in all white, with a perfectly trimmed beard the size of a human hand. He was sitting on a stool with a display of literature and books, with his back to the street. He was facing an open door building from which cooler air seemed to originate before being sucked out to the sidewalk on the passersby. The man was much older than me and thin, but he had a very gentle face and kind eyes. I stopped and began speaking with the man, browsing the various books with Claudette. The books were all written in English and they were all about different aspects of Islam. As we spoke, the man told me I could choose any book he had, at no charge. I was taken back at this offer because it was very generous.

As I looked over the books, I had a difficult time making a decision because there were so many that I would find interesting. I finally decided on a book that was entitled, *Atlas of the Koran*, a book about the spread of Islam, the battles and their prophets and leaders. Without being aware of my surroundings and without looking up, I said, "Sir, I would like to have this one but I am willing to pay you for it." I knew he was going to give it to me, but I thought it would be a nice gesture to offer.

From behind me I heard an emphatic "NO." As I turned, another man was behind me; he was younger, as tall as I was, which was odd because most Saudis are shorter than Americans. This man had the same outfit and perfectly trimmed beard and he had come from the cool area off the sidewalk. I then realized that these were the Mutawwa and they were trying to evangelize people for Islam.

These two men were insistent; they would take no money at all. Both spoke freely about their faith and assumed I was a Christian – but never made a negative remark about Christianity. Even though they were part of the Mutawwa and had probably taken part in the execution of "infidels" like me, they were very kind and gracious.

The younger man took the lead in the conversation. He offered me the very gracious privilege to take from him any book from that table that I found interesting. As our conversation went forward, he probed what my interests were and then suggested a book from the collection. I thought to myself, "Why don't we do this as Christians? This is an outstanding tool to use for Christ; find out what a person's interests are then give them literature centered around that particular interest." Later, I would find that this man was accurate in his suggestions because the books he suggested were indeed very interesting.

Mr. Mutawwa, as I have come to refer to him, had only one "catch" to his offer. He would give me any book I wished provided he could give a gift to my wife. He was speaking of Claudette, who was still just wearing the abaya. It was normal for him to assume that she was my wife because it is illegal for a man to be in public with a woman other than his wife. In his mind, 'Why would anyone approach the Mutawwa while breaking the law?' I'm glad he thought I was a law abiding westerner.

I turned to Claudette and said, "Dear, this gentleman would like to give you something." Realizing who these men were and the fact we both could be arrested, she quickly caught on and said, "Certainly. Whatever you wish." Our hosts who were really married and who had watched us minister for several months, thought this was hilarious and turned away trying not to blow our cover once again with their laughter.

The younger man, Mr. Mutawwa, handed me a book and said, "Please, for your wife." Saudi men do not address nor have one-on-one contact with any woman other than a close family member; in their culture, this is how you respect wives and daughters of other men. In Arabic, I thanked him; but that was the extent of my Arabic, and I switched to English thanking him again for his kindness. I turned to my new "wife," who respectfully stood behind me, looking at the ground, and handed her the book we had received. It was a book designed for women only, explaining the virtues as to why women should always keep their faces veiled except for their husbands. That night, I read that book cover to cover. I found that the book wasn't as much about veiling the face as it was about a woman keeping her purity for her husband.

Mr. Mutawwa had given me 15 books or more and he tried to give me others, but I didn't want to take advantage of the situation. I have read several of the books and they are very interesting. While there are great theological divides concerning grace, salvation, the nature of Jesus Christ and several other issues, I can honestly say that the Muslim has a tremendous grasp on the holiness of God, something many American Christians lack. The only problem is that they attempt to serve what they do not know, resulting in a horribly misguided and misinformed faith while remaining hopelessly lost. As to their concepts and reasons as to why they do much of what they do religiously, I can honestly say that I understand their reasoning behind their actions, but I do not agree with them.

Throughout the day we had many experiences and an excellent time, and it did boost our morale as intended. I bought Arabic swords for my nephews and son, jewelry boxes for my nieces and daughter and a black Islamic outfit for my wife. I thought that was quite humorous; she did not share in my laughter. I even bought an ice-cream cone at a Baskin Robbins in Riyadh; it cost me a quarter.

As the sun began to set over the Arabian Desert, we drove back to base and I realized a truth about people on this planet. For the most part, the men and women that occupy this earth are generally the same in most respects. We have different languages and cultures, sometimes causing great divides in our thinking and understanding; but generally speaking, we are truly more alike than we are different. I discovered that the average Saudi Muslim was very much like me, an average Christian American. He loves his family, his friends and his faith; he wants to live in safety and to be free. He is not a terrorist at all; most of all, he wants the mercy of God in his life. And this perhaps, is the saddest thing about him. For though he desires the mercy and grace of God, he may never receive it or hear about it because evangelism in the name of Jesus Christ is forbidden by the government, punishable by death; and it is Jesus alone by which men must be saved.

Chapter 10

It Ain't Over, Till it's Over

On April 25, 1915, the Australian-New Zealand Army Corps (ANZAC) stormed the beaches of Gallipoli in an effort to knock the Ottoman Empire out of World War I and alleviate pressure on the Allies from the combined efforts of the Central Powers. This operation would also help the Allies gain control of the Dardanelles, which secured passage into the Mediterranean Sea. The ANZACs were met with overwhelming firepower and were bogged down in a stalemate of armies which lasted eight months. In the end, both sides suffered tremendous casualties throughout the campaign and ultimately, the ANZAC force lost the engagement as the people of Australia and New Zealand had lost nearly a generation of young men. Lest we forget.

As April neared an end and my date to rotate out of the theatre neared, both my commander and I were contacted through the appropriate channels via the United States Embassy about a request for my presence at the Australian Embassy to conduct and take part in their celebrations of ANZAC Day. It was at this time I was told that not only was I the only chaplain in KSA for the U.S. military, but I was also considered the Coalition Chaplain for all Allied forces in that region of the theatre. In short, I was being "voluntold" to take part in this special celebration. In truth, no one had to "tell" me to do this; being asked to join our Coalition Allies in their special day was truly an honor. In global politics, there are allies and friends; Australia has been a good friend of the United States and our troops around the globe for many years. There was no question in my mind; I would do whatever they needed me to do on ANZAC Day.

Chaplain Jack, Col. Mike Hatcher and Australian Ambassador

I met with the Australian Defense Attaché at their embassy. While I had done some research on the ANZAC, the first order of business was for me to find out who they were and what they did. He described their actions in a story of gallantry, bravery and honor. The ANZACs are revered by the Australians for their courage during the Great War. All around the globe on April 25th, every year, Australians and New Zealanders hold celebrations beginning at dawn. Generally, the same format and events take place. There are prayers, speeches, Scripture readings, hymns and the laying of wreaths. Regardless of where a person is located in the world, the same order of service is usually followed. Make no mistake – this was a religious service, which is why they requested my presence.

I was informed that after the service there would be what they referred to as a "Gunfire Breakfast." I had no clue as to what this was, but it was modeled after what many of the ANZACs ate in the field. A Gunfire Breakfast consisted of home-made biscuits, rum and milk. Captain Murray Gordon (Australian Air Force) was a wonderful host. He said I should think of ANZAC Day as the American Veteran's Day, Independence Day and Memorial Day all wrapped into one celebration, and described as their D-Day. What I didn't understand was why there was such a celebration since they had lost. It didn't make sense to me because Americans don't celebrate war time losses. For example, we do not have an "Alamo Day," or a "Little Big Horn Day." Captain Gordon's answer was simple: Australia and New Zealand had been independent nations for about 10 years when the ANZACs took the field. Their prolonged fight gave both nations world-wide legitimacy and established them on the map.

I left the meeting with a better understanding of what was to take place and why. Captain Gordon presented me a gift on that day, which is a traditional gesture among military men, although I didn't realize this at the time. He gave me a very nice pen and letter opener set held in a carved block of wood with the Australian Air Force Emblem built into the front of it. The letter opener is in the shape of a ceremonial Australian military sword. I was very grateful for this gift and it remains one of my prized possessions from the desert as it sits on my desk to this day.

The ANZAC celebration was to take place outdoors at Sunrise at their embassy. In the darkness of Eskan, Colonel Hatcher and I left the base and arrived at the embassy just before dawn. It was 90 degrees before the sun rose. As we entered, Captain Gordon's assistant was handing out poppies, which is a memorial symbol of their people. Traditionally, they are placed on the lapel over the individual's heart. Colonel Hatcher and I placed them on our uniforms and then made our way into the assembly area.

Stepping through the doors, we could sense a very somber atmosphere, but the place was packed with people from all over the world. The majority were military men from around the globe; some were our allies and some were our adversaries. Each of them, along with their nation's ambassador, had been sent to Saudi Arabia to advance their homeland's agenda with the host nation.

At the outdoor location of the Australian Embassy where the celebration was to take place, stood several large Gum trees which are native to Australia and much larger than those found in America. One thing that was not mentioned was the fact that these particular Gum trees tend to attract flies. I have conducted services, preached and prayed in locations that were too hot, too cold, too boring, too loud and various other difficulties; but this is the only time I have ever led a service where the congregation and the speakers were attacked by swarms of insects.

For several days prior, I had met with one of my very gifted singers from the Chapel; I needed him to teach me how to lead and sing the old hymn "Abide with Me." I would be leading the singing of this hymn at the ANZAC service and I was concerned, but I thought I could get through it just fine because there would be music to drown out my pitiful singing voice. My friend taught me the best he could and I was thankful; however, ten minutes before the service, I was informed that there would be no music for the hymn. Now, I am many things, but I have never claimed to be a singer and without music being played, I realized I needed my church choir more than ever. With a few adaptations, we made it through the song. Leading that song happens to be the longest three minutes of my entire life.

On the platform I sat with Captain Gordon and the Ambassadors from Australia, Britain, New Zealand and Turkey. I wondered what Turkey's ambassador would say because it was his nation that had won the engagement so many years before. He was very respectful and shared the sober attitude of those who had lost the ANZAC.

It came time for the reading of Scripture and message, which was John 15:9-14:

'Jesus said, "As the Father has loved me, so I have loved you. Dwell in my love. If you heed my commandments, you will dwell in my love, as I have heeded my Father's commands and dwell in his love.

I have spoken thus to you, so that my joy may be in you, and your joy complete. This is my commandment: love one another, as I have loved you. There is no greater love than this, that someone should lay down his life for his friends.""

Messages preached at such events are commonly called 'God and Country' sermons by preachers and pastors. Personally, I have a difficult time preparing special day messages because expectations are usually higher on special days (Christmas, Easter, Mother's Day, etc.) than at any other time of the year. This particular special day was even more difficult because it was to be a 'God and Country' message, but only three-quarters of the people there believed in the same God as I did and only two of us were from America. While this was a difficult service in the desert, it was also one of the most rewarding.

Throughout the service I knew near the end a recording would be played of the national anthems, "Advance Australia Faire" and "God Defend New Zealand." I wondered what the protocol was for such a situation; I didn't know if I was supposed to salute at our Coalition Allies' national anthems. When the time came and the music played, I kept my eye on Colonel Hatcher. As he began raising his arm to salute, so did I. Later, I asked him about this and he said that he really didn't know what we were suppose to do either, but he knew "it couldn't hurt." It didn't. In fact, the Australians were quite pleased that Americans were the only people in that service who honored their nation with them.

The last part of the service was to sound "Last Call" and lay the wreaths in the appropriate place to honor those of the ANZAC. Then I stood, gave the benediction, and with that the ANZAC Day services were completed. We were asked to take part in the Gunfire Breakfast. Colonel Hatcher had privately made it clear to me prior to our arrival that I was to take the lead at the embassy and he would follow any decision I made because I had dealt with our Australian counterparts more than anyone else. While I longed for a real home-made biscuit, somehow eating it with the concoction of rum and milk mixed together just did not appeal to me. Knowing that Colonel Hatcher had "commander" type of things to do that were far more important than what most people realized, I politely declined the offer. If I had been alone, I may have stayed a while, if only to speak with some of our allies in uniform.

As we left, the assistant to Captain Gordon stopped me. John Shank had driven me many times to the Australian embassy; while I was talking with their people and setting up the services, Shank just waited in their library or spent time talking with Gordon's female assistant. On this day, Shank didn't go into the embassy; he remained outside and waited on guard in the vehicle. The assistant must have been quite taken with Shank, for she was disappointed that she wouldn't get to see him that day. She handed me a gift especially for him. If John Shank were married, I would have never breathed a word of it.

The entire experience was enjoyable, but also very sobering. Amid the prayers, bugle sounds, speeches and the laying of wreaths, I believe there was a moment when most everyone recognized and realized that the men of the ANZAC were a symbol and the forerunners of what was to come. They died in what was called, "The War to End All Wars;" however, the twentieth-century proved to be a time when mankind nearly perfected the art of warfare; killing and destroying more human life than at any other time in the history of the world. The ANZACs sacrificed themselves for the cause of freedom and liberty, a cause and a belief that is still worth fighting for today. They are a reminder, as are the men and women circling the globe this hour, that liberty is not a privilege given by a government to its subjects; liberty is a human right, a gift given by the hand of Almighty God. Lest we forget.

Chapter 11

Odds and Ends

With any good tale, there are always odd, interesting and even exciting facts that occur, but they don't always fit with the rest of the story. Such was the case with my time in the desert. What follows is a collage of mostly unrelated experiences, questions I have been asked since returning and the like. Each helps to complete the story of my tour of duty at Eskan Village Air Base, Kingdom of Saudi Arabia.

Armed Forces Network (AFN) has been bringing military men and women broadcasts of radio and television shows for many years. What most people do not realize is that AFN contains no commercials. AFN is a free service to the military and is non-profit, with no broadcast airtime sold to advertisers. The networks or groups who own the rights to the show or event, such as the NFL or Major League Baseball, donate the programs to AFN. Yet, there are time gaps of what normally would be commercial breaks; so, something must fill up that gap of time in the broadcast. During these breaks, AFN airs something similar to public service announcements geared toward the military. While occasionally there would be a historic fact or information about the various state capitols, most of the topics were on issues such as alcoholism, overcoming drug addictions, how to respond to sexual harassment, how to get out of an abusive relationship and other negative stereotypical issues. AFN ran so many of these "spots" on the air that it would lead you to believe most of our service people are abusive, alcoholic, sexually harassing gamblers whose lives are out of control. And at the end of every one of these ads, the message on the screen would always suggest that the afflicted should "contact the chaplain." It then occurred to me why chaplains are always needed in the military and why we are so overworked.

Along with AFN there were other television channels that must have been purchased or owned by the Saudi government. These channels did have commercials, but they weren't like American commercials. For example, an American diaper commercial shows women with babies doing motherly types of things. In KSA, the commercials would show men with babies and the babies were always clothed. If the channel was from another country, such as Bahrain (which is more liberal in their beliefs) you might actually see a female without a veil. And sometimes you might see a commercial three different times on various channels with three different languages dubbed with voice-overs.

Regardless of the origin of the channel, the Saudi censors were ever on the alert to blur any unacceptable body parts that might be showing. For example, one night I was flipping through the channels and discovered MTV-Europe. On the station was a famous American female singer, dancing and presumably in little clothing. Her entire body was blurred out except for her head, feet and hands. I found this cultural difference quite amusing.

Another thing I found humorous was the fact that I was often mistaken for a Saudi national. In both flying into and out of Saudi Arabia, the flight attendants never offered me alcohol and both times they served me Halal meals. These meals are for adherents of Islam and strictly follow Muslim dietary laws. In country, several times men began speaking to me in Arabic, a mistake on their part, which served me well at times.

Most Americans look at the cultural standards and norms of Saudi Arabia and naturally compare them to ours in the United States. Quite honestly, it is like comparing apples to oranges. The one thing that does stand out, other than the form of government, is the treatment of Saudi Arabian women. Most Americans will look at their way of life and conclude that Saudi women are devalued, degraded, oppressed and in need of liberation. Believe it or not, they think the same thing about American women. In fact, many Saudis believe that American men place very little value on their wives and daughters. I discovered this when speaking with a member of the Saudi Arabian National Guard.

Saudi women stick out like a sore thumb because they are covered head to toe in black; they are veiled and some even wear black gloves. I asked the guardsman why this was a law and why women couldn't speak in public to men. His answer was simple: "protection." He explained that the dress protected them from the sun, which made sense but this was extreme. He then said it also protected them from "the lustful wiles of wicked men." I could also understand this point. With no revealing clothes, no speaking to men who are not your husband and a man not speaking to a woman who wasn't his wife, there is little chance either could flirt or send the wrong impressions to a member of the opposite sex.

The King's chief duty was to help his people become better Muslims as he protected the two holiest shrines of Islam. These particular rules were strictly followed and they were for the protection of a family's honor and the female's dignity. Privacy was also very important. Walls are built around dwellings, keeping family issues safe and private. When a person violated this privacy or the honor of a female, they were severely punished. For example, I was delayed in country because my replacement did not arrive on time. During that same week, a man was caught attempting to rape a woman on Sunday; he was executed on Friday.

While I am certain not all Saudis view these practices imposed on them as justified in protecting their honor, and some do use it to oppress and dominate the women of that country, I am equally certain that many truly believe and practice these traditions. In most cases, the family and its female members are held in the highest esteem.

I have been asked about what type of activities we did in the desert during our down time. Personally, after sermon preparation or visitation, I watched a lot of TV and read a lot of books, especially after I was injured and immobilized. Before I was injured, I did what everybody else did for fun – used the Morale, Welfare and Recreation (MWR) facilities and programs. The base had several hardened tents with top of the line exercise equipment and weights available. We also had organized sports such as softball, aerobics, yoga and basketball. There were also four libraries on base with books, movies and music. Some who are deployed get in a routine and then they find themselves getting in a rut; which is usually followed by struggles with depression. I never had this problem because I was always busy except for late at night. Being the only chaplain in the country, I had little time to get bored because the ministry demands were so high. In this respect, I was very blessed to be very busy.

I have nothing but good things to speak about the USO. Along with the Miami Dolphin Cheerleaders, they brought to us comedy acts and musicians. One music act was the band called "Los Bad Apples." I met them one morning while they were using the WiFi at the Chapel office; we had established this as a morale booster for the troops. I was able to speak at length with the band and found they were very intelligent and well mannered, which was not the impression a person would have at first glance. Their music was blend of Mexican rhythm, Hip Hop and Heavy Metal; this seemed like a very odd mixture and not very appealing to me personally – organ music is more my style. Therefore, I skipped their shows. Weeks later, TSgt Tonya Cabellero gave me a CD of the Los Bad Apples. I did not listen to the CD until I came home, and to my surprise, they were very good. They were so good and talented, that I now regret not going to their shows.

MWR and Services had something going on nearly everyday of the deployment. They combined budgets and manpower, putting on tournaments of Texas Hold 'em, ping pong, dominoes and Bingo once a month. It amazed me as to how many people would play Bingo, but I soon found out the reason – the prizes were excellent.

Playing Bingo, I won several good prizes. The most valuable prizes to me were two stuffed camels that I sent home to my children. The camels play a children's song in Arabic, which is unique, but they are important to me because my kids have enjoyed them so much. One night, I was given a five-minute crash course in Dominoes, which I had not played except for one time with my father years before. I won the tournament that night, along with another camel, which I sent to my Associate Pastor's daughter.

The Associate Pastor of my home church, West Ripley Baptist, is Franklin Howerton. While I was in the desert, Franklin took care of most of the preaching and nearly all of the pastoral issues at West Ripley. He, my wife and church family conspired not to tell me anything that was happening in the church; they filtered all information. In short, I had no idea what was going on in the church back home. This was a wise move because no matter what information I would have received, I would have worried about it, but there was no need for me to worry at all. When I returned home and went to church on Sunday morning, I stood before the congregation and noticed a lot of new faces that I didn't recognize. As it turned out, not only had God's Spirit been moving in the desert, but He had moved at West Ripley as well. Seven new believers had been baptized since I had left; more had joined the church and attendance had grown. Some ministers worry when they step out for several months about what will happen or who will take over, but I never did. I am so thankful for what God did on both sides of the globe through our ministries during that time; I am more thankful that I am serving alongside a true man of God.

The King of the Desert is a title given to a man who comes to Eskan Village about every six months. He arrives with camels, falcons and food. He lets the troops play with the falcon, ride the camels and then he feeds the troops; the only catch was that you had to listen to his speech about converting to Islam. That wasn't a problem for me because I truly wanted to ride a camel and eat authentic Arabian food; I had grown to like it.

A camel has two sets of knees, one in the front of the leg and one in the rear; they fold and collapse the leg like a hydraulic jack. While on the camel, he decided he was hungry and collapsed his legs to the ground, nearly throwing me off. It wasn't until that time that I realized how big a camel truly is, how high a person was off the ground on its back, and how mean and nasty they truly are. The beast nearly flung me into the hard sand, but who was I to tell a camel when he can and cannot eat? I just hung on for dear life as the troops took pictures of my fearful expressions.

Claudette and I hosted several social events/fellowship times on the roof of the chapel office; the prayer garden and fountain located on the roof made for a nice atmosphere. In Saudi, American restaurants have an Arab flavor about them. A customer can order what he would order here and what he will receive will be similar, but not exact. One night, I had one of the permanent party men to go off base to a local Pizza Hut because nobody had eaten Pizza Hut pizza for months. We thought this would be a nice treat for the troops. That night was the only time in my life that I have eaten pizza with pepperoni made from goat meat. Like I said, similar but not exact; it was good, but it was also just a little different.

One day, Rick and Nancy Jackson's daughter and her family came for a visit from the United States. Nobody in the chapel services knew they were coming. When they came to the Friday morning services, every eye turned to them because they had brought their children with them. Not one person in that room had been around nor seen a child in months. As the service began, I welcomed everyone but then turned to them and informed them that after the service we would all be going to their villa to play with their grandchildren. Of course we didn't, but every person in that room wanted to.

No story is complete without a legend, and Eskan Village has one of its own. There was a place on base, which was off-limits to most people, called the "Exclusion Zone." We also called it Vampire Land because of the massive number of bats in that area. In that area of the base, there is a building called the Schwarzkopf Building. A strong rumor testified that it was from this building that General Norman Schwarzkopf ran the Persian Gulf War against the aggression of Sadaam Hussein. At some point during the tour, Eskan was visited by a retired general officer who had been on Schwarzkopf's staff during the war. When he came, there was an Airman's Call, meaning, every member of the Air Force on base was to attend his speech. After his speech, he opened it up for questions. One man asked about this building and if the rumor was true. The retired general smiled and told us that it was just a rumor. The fact was there were many more hardened tents on base back then and they ran the war from one of those tents. He also said that General Schwarzkopf never stayed at the base; he was mostly in downtown Riyadh working with the Saudi military during the war. But what happened to the tents utilized in the war from which Sadaam was defeated? Only a handful remained – one of which was the Oasis of Peace Chapel.

Chapter 12

Going Home

"I don't think we're going to make it on time." These were the words I heard from 7,000 miles away in Missouri. It was my replacement giving me a grim notification two days before I was to leave Eskan Village and go home. His words didn't exactly thrill me, but he had not angered me either; I was mostly disappointed because I had hoped to make it home on Mother's Day, surprising my wife during the church service.

Chaplain Marty Clary was my replacement and he was concerned about his situation; maybe more so than I at the time. I believed that it would all work out in the end. The new chaplain had problems with receiving a visa to enter the Kingdom. He had a passport and sent it for clearance to the State Department, who would then forward it to the Saudi Arabian embassy for visa approval. His home station had sent his documents with plenty of time to spare, but they sent it to the wrong address thereby never gaining a visa or clearance to enter the country, while at the same time losing his passport. In all likelihood, I was told, it would take a three-month turnaround period before his passport and visa application could be approved.

TSgt Arms was in the same situation as I. Although her replacement was coming from a different home station than Chaplain Clary, her home station had done the exact same thing and her paperwork was also lost in the process. The difference between Claudette and myself was the fact that I had to get her home on time. In the real world, TSgt Claudette Arms is a school teacher and had to get back to her civilian job. At that time I began calling all the right people in theatre to get her out of the country. The Commander of the base approved her departure without question, as did Command Chaplain Bristol once I explained the situation. After sending Claudette to the logistics people, the next day she was on her way out of Saudi Arabia and headed for home.

As I talked with Chaplain Bristol, he asked me what I wanted to do, which I found odd, so I asked what he meant. He said guardsmen have a dual mission: a federal mission like all military members, but also a state mission. Guardsmen can be federalized, as when activated, but our time on active duty is usually limited unless we are extended. There are only two ways to extend – the guardsman volunteers and gets the appropriate approval, or by order of the Secretary of the Air Force acting on the behalf of the President. Chaplain Bristol did not have that authority and explained to me the three options available.

The simplest option would be to stay in theatre until my scheduled replacement arrived; that could be a 60 to 90 day extended stay at Eskan Village. The second option was that I could simply leave theatre without being replaced; it takes a while to get clearance to enter the country and very few chaplains actually had clearance. Since there was no replacement immediately available, no chaplain would replace me and I could just leave. The third option was that I could stay until a chaplain who had clearance from a previous rotation could be mobilized and sent back to Eskan Village. Once they arrived I could leave at that time. None of these three options sounded appealing to me.

After all God had done at Eskan while I was ministering there, I couldn't just leave the people without another chaplain taking my place. I was not going to abandon the chapel community, it just wouldn't be right. I also thought it wasn't right to ask a previous chaplain to return to KSA; I was already there and there was no reason for me to inconvenience my predecessors. For a week I had began turning my heart and mind back to the home front, but I decided while on the phone with Chaplain Bristol that my fond ideas of reuniting with those back home would have to wait. I softly said to Chaplain Bristol, "I am prepared to stay here for an additional 60 to 90 days until I am replaced; but I don't think I'll be able to stay any longer than 90."

Chaplain Bristol sounded a little surprised, but he also sounded appreciative. From his perspective, this was the end of the problem; no further attention to it was necessary. The chaplain slot at Eskan would remain filled, and as he was nearing his departure date to leave theatre, the next command chaplain could deal with this situation.

During this time, many on base had great joy at my expense. I had been counting down the days, as everyone does, as to when I would leave. That countdown was now abruptly stopped. As of that moment, I would be staying in theatre longer than many of those who were on the normal six-month rotation cycle. We had some fun with it, but I really couldn't laugh too much about it or get carried away with any emotions because I had to prepare for the next chapel service, only this time, I had no assistant to help me. I also had to prepare for the bi-weekly visit of a Catholic chaplain from another base, and with deep appreciation to God's guiding hand and Providence it was Chaplain Dan Bergbower.

Chaplain Bergbower and I formed a wonderful friendship in the desert. He had spent several tours ministering throughout the theatre and had achieved the rank of Lieutenant Colonel. He was also a member of the Air National Guard and knew the ins and outs of desert ministry. When I told him what was happening, he said that I needed to contact the National Guard Bureau (NGB) and tell them what was happening because ultimately, I fell under their authority. My contact at NGB was Chaplain (Major) Sarah Shirley. I emailed her and informed her what was going on at Eskan and from the email I received in return, I could immediately tell she was not a happy camper. When I emailed her, I did it from the perspective of "this is what is happening and I have accepted it." When she returned my email, this was not her attitude at all. To her, this was not an acceptable situation. She informed me that she would get the replacements to Eskan Village ASAP, and ultimately, she did.

Chaplain Shirley contacted the Guard Bases of both the chaplain and his assistant and used her authority to have them on the next flight leaving the areas to Washington, D.C. Both of them arrived at the same time. It is my understanding that Chaplain Shirley met them at the airport then physically escorted them to the State Department where they received new passports. Afterwards, they headed to the Saudi Arabian embassy where they received clearance and visa approval to enter the Kingdom. The next day, the replacements were on their way to Eskan Village. Instead of 60 to 90 days, it turned out to be a delay of only one week. I wish all areas of government were this efficient.

When the replacements did arrive in country, they were several hours late in making it to the base. There was some type of mix-up at the airport and were delayed. SSgt John Shank had picked them up; upon dropping them off, he said, "Have fun." From his expression, they must have had a horrible time getting them through customs. It looked as if he had all that he could have taken in dealing with the new arrivals.

Just as when I had arrived, there were a couple of other people with them. Originally, the parking lot was full awaiting their arrival, but due to the fact that they were delayed for hours, it had dwindled to only a handful of us. In any case, we knew that they would be hungry once they eventually got there, so we had gone to the DFAC before the hot line stopped serving and gathered up food for them. After quick introductions, we walked over to the chapel office where they could eat in relative peace. After welcoming them to Eskan and talking about their flight, we took the new assistant to her villa and we retired to ours.

It is a tradition among the chaplains serving at Eskan Village to move out of the chaplain's room when the replacement arrived. Chaplain Clary was surprised and thrilled, just as I had been five months earlier. The next morning when I saw him, I could tell he had experienced a miserable night, but I didn't know why. As it turned out, the air conditioning unit in the 'chaplain's room' decided to die; instead of knocking on my door or sleeping in another room, he sweltered in misery all night long. I taught him how to contact the right people and showed him whom he would need to talk to get it fixed and it was fixed that day, much to his delight.

A day earlier, when Eskan was notified that he would be arriving, logistics began working to get me out of the country. Unknown to me, there was a large body of replacements arriving for the next rotation. Logistics would have to get me on a plane before they arrived or I would have to wait another one to two weeks before I could leave. The reason was because the SET team could not escort these large groups of replacements to the base while at the same time escorting individuals to commercial flights; they did not have the manpower. That meant Chaplain Clary and I would have only two full days together for a transition, half the time of my transition period when I arrived.

Claudette had left several days earlier and I was concerned about being able to help the new chaplain assistant understand her responsibilities. I greatly underestimated Claudette. We had been working on continuity binders for several weeks, but I had never looked at hers until her replacement arrived. It was nearly perfect. Everything that I didn't know and all of what I did know about the chaplain assistant's job was in that binder. Once again, Claudette had risen above the call of duty and made our chapel team shine.

At first Chaplain Clary seemed worried; he had many questions and concerns, but I assured him that he had nothing to worry about. Most things at Eskan naturally fall into place because of the strong chapel community. In time, he would realize this and be blessed by them. The simple truth is that a chaplain from the civilian world already knows how to do ministry; all he really needed was to be taught how to work and file the Air Force mandatory forms, and it doesn't take much time to show someone how to type in a number on a sheet of paper and then email it to Higher Headquarters.

As Chaplain Clary settled into his new role, the time had come for me to take a step back and let go of the reins of ministry at Eskan Village. LTC Wagner's replacement was about to have his change-of-command ceremony; Wagner asked if I would give the invocation. I had done many ceremonies of this nature in the desert, but I had not planned for this one. I thought the new chaplain should do it because my time was ending; but it was a personal request from a man who had become a dear friend. I simply could not refuse; it would be my last official act as the chaplain of the 64th AEG. LTC Wagner became a bookend of my ministry in the desert; his incoming and outgoing ceremonies were the first and last ministry events I was involved with at Eskan Village. For the remainder of my time, following Wagner's advice, I stepped into the shadows and let go of the ministry and the people I had come to love in a very short amount of time. While it was difficult to let go of something so special, it was necessary; my time had come to an end and the charge of ministry had been fulfilled in a powerful way.

As the days at Eskan drew to a close, some wonderful things happened to me. Before I left for the desert, a person at my church had confiscated my Bible and had my congregation write messages on the blank pages in the front. One even included a hand-written note and tucked it away among the pages. Those messages became very special to me as I read them in the desert; some were prayers, others were simple well wishes, but all provided some type of encouragement to me when I needed it the most. Before I left Eskan, each one of my chapel congregations did the same thing, only they wrote their messages on the blank pages in the back. From time to time, I open those pages and read them, always being encouraged in remembering how God moved in the desert. Quite possibly the most humbling thing was that they had written about how God touched them through me, and the fact that they did not call me "chaplain." They referred to me as their "pastor."

Throughout the last week, even before Chaplain Clary arrived, the chapel community blessed me in many ways. Many of them invited me to their villas for home-cooked meals. Some gave gifts of appreciation and thanks. The believers at the embassy held a going away party for me. All of these small events were meaningful in a pastoral way; I knew they loved me and were thankful God had chosen me to be among them.

Before the Believers at the Breezeway in my last chapel service, I stood in front of them and told them that chaplains don't usually get coins or medals for what they do; seeing the ministry take place and lives changed was our reward. I made it a point to tell them it had been, "an honor and a privilege to have been called as your chaplain and to minister among you during this time." I meant every word from the bottom of my heart. The chapel community applauded and I choked back a few tears as many were beginning to get emotional – until General Van Sickle stood up and interrupted the service. He walked forward, publicly expressed his appreciation and gratitude for my work and then handed me his commander's coin. That was unexpected and I was thankful I had been wrong. In total, I received 11 coins from different people; 4 of them were "commander coins" from different commanders. I was also recommended for the Air Force Commendation Medal. These are high honors and almost unheard of in the chaplain field; I am still humbled to know these men and women thought so highly of me and appreciated the Spirit's work through me.

My last meal at Eskan was a "Going Home" dinner at the DFAC. All the commanders were there, as were most of the officers and senior enlisted airmen. They had pooled their money together and bought me what is called a "camel saddle," which is an Arabian footstool. I had already packed, so they had it shipped to my house in West Virginia. It sits in my home at this very moment.

CHAPLAIN JACK MILLER ON ROOFTOP

The DFAC parking lot was full of people on the night I left. Seven others were leaving on the same flight, all of us heading in different directions once we made it to Europe. I felt very odd knowing that I was seeing these men and women for the last time. Pictures were taken for the last time; there were hugs and handshakes and small good-byes. The last thing I did was to shake Chaplain Clary's hand and say a quick prayer for him and his ministry in the desert. With that, I loaded my gear into a van, sat down in the seat and left Eskan Village Air Base, Kingdom of Saudi Arabia.

Epilogue

The flights and transitions had gone well; only one of the seven other men who left the Kingdom with me remained. Each had gone their own directions with various connecting flights. At Dulles International, the last of the men left me to go his own route to New York. Walking through the airport was much different now than it had been five months prior. I was darker, in uniform, and very weary; I had not slept in 41 hours.

As I waited for the time when my flight to Charleston, West Virginia was to board, I saw a coffee stand. For the first time in five months I paid for a cup of coffee. It wasn't the greatest in the world, but it was much better than the gasoline I had been drinking in the desert.

In the terminal I saw a man wearing a World War II veteran ball cap. I walked over to him and knelt down, thanking him for his service, and he thanked me for mine. As we talked, I asked him what theatre he was in during WWII. He told me he had been in the Middle East working among the Arabs against the Nazi threat. I told him I had just come from Saudi Arabia, my unit working with Arabs trying to eliminate the threat from Al-Qaida. It struck us both odd that our tours were separated by nearly 70 years and the mission in the desert was not yet accomplished, quite possibly because the enemy is so vastly different today than it was back then.

The flight to Charleston was rough, but I was taken by the beauty of the mountains, greenery and clouds; I had seen none of these things in months. Mostly, I just stared out the window wondering how God was going to use this experience. Upon landing and the engines shutting off, I heard a voice behind me say, "Welcome home, Captain." His voice was followed by others on the plane. The same uneasiness I had felt in the parking lot at Eskan Village quickly returned.

Immediately after stepping off the plane, I knelt down and thanked God for bringing me home and for what He did through me in the desert. I had not expected Him to move as powerfully or quickly, but He had indeed moved and I am still thankful and humbled by this fact.

In the terminal stood my children, wife, family and church family. They held signs and posters, welcoming me home. The first words out of my mouth were, "So, what's new with you?" They all laughed, but it was my way dealing with my nervousness. I appreciated each of them being there, but I appreciated more the fact they supported me and my ministry throughout the years and through this time of deployment.

In the weeks that followed I thought a lot, probably because I had not been allowed that luxury in the desert. I thought about what had happened, how God might use the experiences and about the future, which caused me to think about my children and my grandchildren they would one day bring home from the hospital. Then I thought to myself, one day my grandchild will climb up on my lap. That child will ask me, "Pap, what did you do in the great Global War on Terror?" When that happens, I am thankful that I will not have to say, "Well, I talked a good fight from the safety of the pulpit." No. Instead, I will hand him these words on these pages and tell him I was called to a place and a people God had prepared for me so that I could witness His Spirit move in a mighty way in the desert.

CPSIA information can be obtained at www.ICGtesting.com

229336LV00004B/2/P